20A4

CW00518488

REBECCA DE SAINTONGE

Born in 1945, Rebecca de Saintonge left school at sixteen to train as a journalist, and worked for the BBC and independent television before running a Fleet Street-based audio visual production unit specialising in Christian education.

Miss de Saintonge comes from a long line of country people from both sides of the Atlantic. Her father, Rolland, a French Canadian, was one of a small group who re-wrote the constitutions of Germany and Austria after World War Two; her mother's family were teachers and farmers in and around Exmoor in Devon.

The author of several books, Rebecca de Saintonge has lived in the Middle East and, more recently, in Zimbabwe, where she ran a small embroidery and lace making co-operative for African women. She and her husband, a minister in the Church of England, now live in Britain.

SPIRE

Rebecca de Saintonge

OUTSIDE THE GATE

A biography of Nico Smith

Copyright © 1989 by Rebecca de Saintonge

First printed in Great Britain 1989

Spire is an imprint of Hodder & Stoughton *Publishers*

British Library Cataloguing in Publication Data

De Saintonge, Rebecca.
Outside the gate: a biography of Nico Smith.
1. South Africa. Anti-apartheid activities.
Smith, Nico
I. Title
322.4'4'0924

ISBN 0-340-49959-1

All rights reserved. No part of this publication may be reproduced or transmitted in any form or by any means, electronic or mechanical, including photocopying, recording or any information storage or retrieval system, without either prior permission in writing from the publisher or a licence permitting restricted copying. In the United Kingdom such licences are issued by the Copyright Licensing Agency, 33–34 Alfred Place, London WC1E 7DP.

Printed in Great Britain for Hodder and Stoughton Limited, Mill Road, Dunton Green, Sevenoaks, Kent by Richard Clay Limited, Bungay, Suffolk. Photoset by Rowland Phototypesetting Limited, Bury St Edmunds, Suffolk.

Hodder and Stoughton Editorial Office: 47 Bedford Square, London WC1B 3DP.

CONTENTS

A WORD OF THANKS

Nico Smith and I would never have been in the same place at the same time had it not been for the efficiency and sense of humour of the Rev. Ivor Jenkins. His self-effacing courage and dedication to a new South Africa were an inspiration.

I would also like to pay a special acknowledgment to David Harrison, for his book *The White Tribe of Africa*, to Wilkins and Strydom for their book *The Super-Afrikaners* and to Dr Sipo Mzimela for *Apartheid: South African Naziism*. These works provided invaluable background information.

Rebecca de Saintonge

PROLOGUE

Smog hangs loosely over the township. It's half past five in the afternoon, the late school-children are lingering home, screwing their eyes against the sudden gusts of wind that whip the pavement into screens of dust. Mothers hurry along, heads down, their babies strapped tightly to their backs in a cocoon of blankets. The air is thick with coal smoke.

Hundreds of men and women swarm from the station and walk home: past the dirt field with its football posts, past the half-burnt piles of garbage, past the late stall-holders with their tiers of red tomatoes, past the gaudy government posters that read WELCOME TO MAMELODI and TOGETHER WE'LL BUILD A BETTER FUTURE, over the potholes in the roadway, past the tiny four-roomed houses, past the wire fences entwined with wild impomoea and past the bleak rows of hostels where men in their thousands are made to live, thick as ants, without their wives, without their children, if they are to work for whites in the comfortable suburbs on the other side of the hill.

The six o'clock sun is a bright red ball hanging in a dense sky. The sounds of the rush hour are beginning to fade. The buses have stopped roaring through the holes in their exhaust pipes. An occasional army tank trundles through the street – young white faces looking blankly out on the settling community. Disco sounds of a nearby beer-hall waft on and off in the wind, neighbours call an evening greeting and from the distant foothills you can hear the faint cry of the dogs.

The people of Mamelodi go to bed soon after dusk and rise long before dawn.

Near the railway station and not far from the Kentucky Fried Chicken there is a small round two-storey house – number 7000 – with a *polygone* roof – looking rather like a tortoise on stilts. It is surrounded by a low brick wall and dusty daisy bushes. Inside live Dr Nico Smith and his wife, Ellen. Dr Smith is a seventh-generation Afrikaner, a former member of the Broederbond – the secretive organisation set up to establish and maintain Afrikaner domination in South Africa – and an erstwhile professor of theology of Stellenbosch University.

His old-fashioned Savile Row suit and ostrich-skin shoes look somewhat out of place in the dirt truck he drives with a careless disregard for halt signs and traffic-lights. While his children agree that their father has never yet had an accident, they suspect the drivers behind him most probably have.

Nico Smith looks like the sort of man who picks up a hammer by the wrong end, yet he has built a mission hospital with his own hands. He has held one of the most prestigious academic posts in the country, yet is haunted by an insecurity so acute that it has made him want to run away. Although he has never failed an exam in his life, he feared every exam, and while his teaching and preaching have changed lives, affected whole communities and contributed to the destabilisation of institutions, he still gets moments of panic at the thought of public speaking.

At his side, always, in every situation, is his wife, Ellen. Even in her 60s Ellen is an unusually beautiful woman. Sometimes her eyes are blue, and sometimes they're green, but by 8pm they are usually closing, try as she might, since she rises with Nico at 4.30 every morning to pray and read before taking the long drive to the black hospital of Medunsa where she is a child psychiatrist.

Nico Smith is the first white Dutch Reformed minister to be given permission to live in a black township since the Group Areas Act of the 50s forbade whites and blacks to live in the same vicinity. Although it was a physical move of only a few kilometres from their white Pretoria suburb, emotionally and spiritually it was, he says, like emigrating, but without the encouraging letters from home.

When he and Ellen left Pretoria it was as if they had left the laager for ever. They left behind their history and their culture, their colleagues, their friends and even, to some extent, their family. They moved outside the gate. They were subjected to bitter abuse, dawn phone calls and vitriolic letters, both privately and in the press.

'Go and live with the kaffirs,' wrote one angry Afrikaner, 'then when they go to shoot the blacks they can shoot you, too.'

Wolfram Kistner wrote in 1963:

The path of Jesus has a distinct downward trend. He took sides with the weak, the sick, the poor and the outcasts – those people in whom the brutality of human beings and their society was manifested. Jesus is a friend of the poor and, strangely enough, lays hold on human society at its bottom end . . .

Whoever wants to live in community with Christ, sustained by his power in this world, can do so only by going outside the gate and becoming one of those people who have nothing to rely on but God's unmerited love and forgiveness.

We are asked to leave behind us everything that gives us false security. We are asked to leave behind us certain criteria which may be accepted in society, where status, merit, achievement and educational qualifications play a role.

In South Africa we need to discern what the term 'outside the gate' means for us.

1

THE BOER PERSPECTIVE

The Afrikaners have always regarded themselves as a persecuted people, and with some reason.

What few British people knew at the time, and few have been taught since, is that during the Boer War 26,000 Afrikaner women and children died in British concentration camps – the first concentration camps the world had ever known.

Even before this, when the British first decided to take over the Cape in the early nineteenth century, they treated the Afrikaners with arrogance and insensitivity, trying to wipe out their newly developing culture and language and crushing all that was 'Afrikaans'.

From the very beginning the Boers felt the English were basically unsympathetic to their cause. Believing themselves to have a God-given responsibility for developing this new South Africa, they resented British sympathy for the black point of view, which they felt was misrepresented and misunderstood.

The British government had consistently refused to help them with their border struggles with the blacks and had taken a hard line over slavery. Boer farmers lost a lot of money when slavery was finally abolished, but the real cause of their anger over the slave issue was not because of the money they lost, but because the British legal system now placed blacks 'on an equal footing with Christians . . . so that it was intolerable for any decent Christian to bow down beneath such a yoke.'

The British government, more interested in the diamonds and gold discovered in such plenty than concern for the blacks (13,000 of whom also died from sickness and malnutrition in the British labour camps of the Boer War), determined to dominate the newly emerging Boer nation.

When they arrived at the Cape at the turn of the century one of their first acts was to suppress the Afrikaans language. Afrikaans had been evolving slowly since the first settlers landed some 200 years before. The High Dutch, from which it originated, was too complicated in its structures for the mixture of races who found themselves living together; there were French, German and Hottentots living side by side with the slaves imported from Malaya and Madagascar, as well as the majority of Dutch.

But the British insisted that English was to be the only language of the courts and, even more significantly, of the schools. There was to be no Afrikaans and no Dutch – this even though the Dutch settlers outnumbered the British by eight to one. For 90 per cent of the rural population virtually all their education was conducted in a language that they had hardly, if ever, heard before. Schoolteachers and school text-books were imported from Britain and the primary-school syllabus was exactly the same as that used in England, even though the everyday imagery was meaningless to children living in Africa.

After the Boer War the pressure to become anglicised became even greater, with children forbidden to speak Dutch or Afrikaans at school, even in the playground. If they were caught they had to wear a placard round their necks for the rest of the day which read, 'I must not speak Dutch'.

One Afrikaans writer later described their education as 'Reading, writing and reckoning, and above all, not speaking Dutch'. However, the children mastered the English language sufficiently to change the words of the British national anthem, which they were forced to sing every morning in school to:

> God save our noble King
> Wash him in paraffin,
> And put fire on him.

So not only did the Afrikaners feel that the British had taken their God-given lands from them and imposed upon them an alien legal and educational system, they had done their best to make the new Boer nation feel inferior. Just as the Afrikaners were struggling to develop a culture and identity of their own, the British had dismantled their emerging cultural structures while scorning them for their lack of cultural identity.

In the same way that 'kaffir' became a habitual term of abuse for the blacks, 'Dutch bastard' was a common derogation on the part of the English. When the South African Broadcasting Corporation introduced its first programmes in Afrikaans, one of the many letters of complaint from an English listener began: 'Dear Enemy,' and went on to accuse them of 'polluting God's clean air with your Afrikaans.'

Nico Smith grew up, like so many Afrikaners before and since, thinking of the British as the oppressor: greedy, imperialistic, arrogant and brutal. Brutal perhaps above all else because his own mother had spent her early years in the concentration camps and watched Nico's grandmother die there.

His mother spoke quite often to the older children about her experiences. She'd been about 7 when her own mother had died – she didn't know what of. But what had frightened her most as a little girl, was the number of children who had died. One of the survivors of the Kroonstad concentration camp, Henning Klopper, verified this when describing his own experience as a small boy to journalist David Harrison.

Klopper's 10-year-old brother had just died of typhoid – which was widespread owing to the poor sanitation in the camps. Not long after one of his sisters became ill, and because there were so few nurses in the camp hospital, she was nursed by another sister. Then that little girl also fell ill as well and it was Klopper's turn to help.

I found her with her arms and legs strapped to the bed. All the others were ill and couldn't visit this sister, they were all in bed. I was the only one that could move.

I came to her bed and saw countless numbers of flies round her face. She couldn't move away from the flies because she was strapped down to the bed. Her mouth was wide open trying to get breath. And the flies were moving in and out of her mouth, her nose and everywhere and there she was, almost in the throes of death with nobody to attend to her, nobody to do anything for her.

I moved away the flies as much as I could but what could I do? I stayed there for possibly an hour, but I was only a little boy. When I told my mother she broke down and was very ill. She couldn't even attend the funeral. I was the only one of the family well enough to go.

And when she was finally dead and they took her off the bed, they found that the bedpan had been under her, possibly for days, because she was all raw underneath.

The English reformer, Emily Hobhouse, who went out to visit the camps, wrote that the whole talk among the inmates was of who had died yesterday and who would die today. The bodies were carried out of the camp at dawn and many buried in mass graves.

It was the deliberate policy of the British government to bring the Boers 'to heel' by rounding up their wives and children. They were shunted by rail to the concentration camps in open coal trucks – four families to a truck, and the journey could take days. There was no proper sanitation or washing facilities on the trucks, and very little water.

Once in the camps food was extremely scarce. Nico's mother would tell them how she and the other children were made to queue sometimes all day in the hot sun for food, only to find when they reached the door of the distribution tent that they were closing it for the day. On those occasions they went back to their families with no food and would have to start again the following morning.

But the story that frightened Nico most when he was a little boy, was about those Boers who had sided with the British. They were regarded by their fellow Afrikaners as sell-outs, fit only to die. The Boer soldiers made them dig their own graves and when they had finished, the 'traitors' were 'shot like dogs', thrown into the holes and buried.

Having rounded up the families of fighting Boers and their black labourers (who were sent to separate work camps and fed even less than the whites), the British soldiers set about destroying everything the Afrikaners had built. Their motive, as expressed by Lord Milner, later British High Commissioner to South Africa, was 'to knock the bottom out of the great Afrikaner nation for ever and ever Amen'. A total of 30,000 farms and 20 villages were razed to the ground; all crops, cattle and buildings were destroyed. They left in their wake total devastation.

When Nico's grandfather eventually came to take his remaining family home from the camp, they found that where their house and farm had been there was nothing but rubble. Everything they owned, even their pots and pans, had been destroyed. There was absolutely nothing left.

So his mother was taken to live with her grandparents, who were wealthy folk, and though she was brought up in fine style – one of the lucky ones – her own life was scarred by her memories of the British which never completely healed.

English was never spoken in Nico's home – it was, after all, the language of the oppressor – and his mother, unbeknown to her husband, was a member of the O.B. (Ossewa Brandwag), an Afrikaans 'cultural' organisation which sabotaged British interests and worked to promote Afrikaner awareness.

Nico's dream, as he grew to maturity, was for a free South Africa, independent of British domination, and he experienced all the euphoria of a liberated people on that day in 1948 when the Afrikaners finally won the general election.

2

AN AFRIKANER CHILDHOOD

The kitchen of the schoolhouse was large enough to eat in. There was a black wood stove in the corner, a dresser with glass doors for the crockery and a scrubbed wooden table where mother and father sat in the evening lamplight pricking the water-melon skins with a fork. Nico's mother made wonderful preserves and the water melon in particular was firm on the outside, but when you bit into it the soft syrupy juices trickled down your chin. You ate the preserves first, and then dipped your bread in the syrup. Nico was the seventh of twelve children, and most of their mother's working day was spent making sure that they were fed.

The pantry in particular held many delights – most of them surreptitiously fingered or licked. There were always jams in season, Cape gooseberry, peach and tomato. There was green-fig preserve and a huge earthenware pot of ginger beer. In the summer Mr Smith would bottle tomatoes from the garden ready for the winter soups.

Three times a week the bread was baked, the brown flour scrupulously sieved so that no trace of bran – which was vulgar – remained. Nico's mother was never vulgar. She could not forget the fact that she was a lady of some social standing in the village, being married to the local schoolmaster, and having once had money of her own.

School was a mornings only affair, and in the afternoons Mum and Dad went to their various parts of the garden, Dad to tend the vegetables, which were his pride and joy, and Mum to the flower garden where she grew dahlias as big as tea-plates. It was while they were out, and the new bread was cooling on the table, that the youngest children would sneak in and hollow the hot dough from the centre of the loaves, leaving only the sides intact, before carefully putting them back under the cooling cloths. This was a regular weekly ritual, but the strange thing is that Mrs Smith never raged about it. She was not an indulgent woman, her own sense of fun having been heavily repressed by poverty and a puritan husband, yet she seemed to accept as part of family life that at least two loaves out of every six would be hollow by teatime. Her revenge came with the weekly dose of cod-liver oil.

It was a family run on routine. Everyone had their chores which had to be done immaculately. Mr Smith would get up first, at about 4.30, to say his prayers and make the freshly-ground coffee. As soon as the aroma reached the younger children they would all begin chanting from their bedrooms, 'We wa-ant coffee. We wa-ant coffee' and up Dad would come with a mug for each child.

Ask any of them now to recall that morning coffee and it's as if they can smell it still, even across the years, because it was more than something to start the day, it was one of their father's few obvious acts of affection that saved their childhood from being too unbearably cold.

When he came home from college during the holidays it was Nico's job to make the morning coffee and it would enrage him to find his baby sister, Sylvia, in bed between mother and father. When the eldest seven were growing up there had been no physical affection at all. No comfort when they fell, no hugs, no kisses, no encouragement to laughter.

'Remember,' their father would say when he heard the children teasing one another, or swinging over the river on a big branch, 'remember, after laughter there are always tears.'

While Dad was downstairs making the morning porridge the children had to make their own beds and the girls were responsible for emptying the potties, each of which had to be scrubbed with Sunlight soap every day and inspected by mother for their cleanliness. There were no inside lavatories of course, and the boys were threatened with everything dire if they dared use their pots in the night. Then the bath had to be cleaned, with its little clawed feet, and the basin. If these jobs were not done properly it was not unlike mother to call the children back from school to do them again – to their everlasting shame.

The boys were responsible for brushing and shining the floors and the youngest, Sarel, Pieter and Jacobus, instead of getting the handbrush, preferred to use their baby sister. They would wrap her in the ironing blanket and run up and down the passage. Bash, bash, bash she'd go against the walls, suppressing her squalls inside the blanket and ending up covered in bruises, the boys warning her not to breathe a word to Mum or Dad. As if she would. It was the highlight of her day.

Mother remained firmly in bed while all this was going on, and only emerged when the dining room was finally laid for breakfast.

When the meal was finished, the prayers began. First Dad would read out of the family Bible, then they would all scrape their chairs back and kneel down, backs to the table. Dad would pray for about ten minutes for the day and bring before God each of his children by name. The children in the meantime would be peeking at each other under the table and making faces. This was strictly forbidden and after prayers someone was bound to say, 'Da-ad, Barbara opened her eyes during the prayers,' and Dad would listen gravely, but say nothing.

In the Afrikaans family, the main meal was always at midday. Despite their poverty, it was always meat, as the farmers kept their schoolmaster well supplied. Afrikaans cooking has been greatly influenced by the Malayans who originally came as slaves and introduced their spices into the local cuisine. The orange pumpkins would be cooked with sugar and cinnamon, the meat well flavoured with cloves. On Sundays, two types of meat were always served – usually mutton and chicken – frequently followed by Nico's favourite spiced dumplings in syrup which he called 'tummy bombs' because they plummeted to the pit of your stomach and rumbled around.

But there were meals eaten that mother knew nothing about; these were the meals cooked by the maid and eaten with the African servants outside under the trees – and as if that wasn't bad enough – eaten with your fingers. These meals would be secretly prearranged with the maids, and the children would eat as little as possible at the table and then dive outside as soon as they decently could. Since their mother was neurotic about them even touching the utensils used by the servants, whom she considered unclean, there is no doubt that these meals, had she known about them, would have triggered off one of her celebrated 'fainting fits' – or worse – which is no doubt partly why they tasted so good.

But despite the fun they had together as children, for many of the twelve their childhood was full of pain. Their mother was a proud, artistic woman who started out in life with high ideals. She had the feeling that she was 'real class' and despite their poverty, she insisted on wearing the best clothes in the neighbourhood and having the best furniture. Where their father found the money, none of them ever knew. But she always struggled with the fact that she had married a poor man. She found it deeply humiliating. Her children had to be wonderfully dressed, even though this meant there was no money left over for toys or for pleasures. Even in her eighties, when she was taken out shopping by her daughters, she would look at the price-tag first to see if the garment was expensive enough to buy.

A schoolmaster's pay was not so bad in those days, but not nearly enough to support such a large family, and Mrs Smith had no say at all in how many children she bore. Her role was to be supportive and submissive. All the major decisions were taken autocratically by the man, and Mr Smith, like many Afrikaners of his day, thought contraception against God's plan.

So the children came along every two years, slowly grinding her down. She would breast-feed them for as long as she could since it was considered ill-mannered for the husband to approach his wife while she was still feeding a child.

Seeing their father's nightly long johns hanging on the line, the early versions of which not only went up to the neck and down to the ankles, but also had no flies, caused both hilarity and amazement among his children, especially the youngest girls (who were a little more liberated in their thinking) as none of them could work out how their father ever managed to sire a child, what with his long johns and their mother's ankle-length nighties.

Not that sex was ever a subject that was talked about among the family. The girls found out about menstruation from one another, not even telling their mother when their periods had started, and the boys stumbled along as best they could, being so inhibited that they didn't even discuss these things among themselves. As a result they picked up the usual weird stories that kids pass on to one another and grew up with a deep sense of guilt at their own sexuality.

Girls remained a mystery to Nico until his university days, and even then he felt that touching them must be sinful. He would indulge in a furtive embrace with a girl from the village, but only because the other boys did, and not because it was much fun, presumably for either of them. But he could never be free with women, and it amazed him that he finally married such a beautiful and emancipated woman.

Talking about her now, after thirty or so years of marriage, he still finds it a miracle that she was willing to accept such an inhibited young man, and that she set him free. He still finds it difficult at times to express his emotions, or to touch, and when Christians began embracing one another in church, 'Boooowwww,' he cries, 'it was so extremely embarrassing for me. I could have died!'

This inability to express love stems largely from his parents who, especially with the older children, were never demonstrative. Father showed by many little practical acts that he loved them. It was he, for instance, who went to them in the night and comforted them if they were frightened, but mother was distant and cold. To this day Nico doesn't know if she ever loved him. She had a real temper, but would leave the punishment to Dad, who out of loyalty to her would beat Nico with a leather strap. The strap was a part of the family equipment and the girls were not infrequently beaten across the shoulders and the boys across the buttocks, and it hurt. But they all knew that their father never beat them aggressively, and often just to satisfy their mother. It made Nico feel both furious and rejected by her. And although as he grew up and achieved well at university she was clearly proud of him, he never in his life communicated with her on any meaningful level, or consciously experienced her love. 'I was softer with my own children,' he recalls, 'but I was always trying to understand how to express love. Emotionally it was the most difficult thing for me to do. Some things I did because I felt you must, it was expected.

'I remember after our children had been through school and university I read a little book by an American child psychiatrist about how really to love your child, and how a child experiences his parents emotionally through physical touch. And I just cried and cried and cried. I couldn't do it, you see, and I didn't understand why I didn't have the capacity to love in this way.' Maybe that is why Nico can be so emotional in his spiritual loving. His relationship with Christ is not cerebral; he experiences it with his whole being. He prays for Christ's presence, and for the Holy Spirit, to flow through his body and mind and will sit back in a chair and allow God to minister to him, without words, and without emotional or intellectual inhibition.

But for Nico and his siblings, all those years ago, guilt was, as Tournier would say, the seasoning of their daily lives. Not just the very personal guilts of a not understood sexuality, but the guilt that comes from not achieving, from not satisfying the high standards laid down, and from the threat of a stern and exacting God.

Mr Smith expected all his children to be top of the class, and to be exemplary in their behaviour. For the bright ones, being top of the class was not much of a problem, and they were all naughty enough privately to be able to put on a reasonable act in public. But not all the twelve survived to tell the tales of their childhood with such ebullience. Two later suffered serious mental stress, one being diagnosed as schizophrenic, and most of them had problematical marriages.

Nico describes his father as a pietistic puritan, and very

legalistic. He believed that you shouldn't really enjoy anything. This was coupled with the old-style German pietism which believed that you couldn't claim to be a child of God unless you had first been through hell-fire and back. A 'real' Christian was one who had struggled with his own inner nature and felt rejected by God because of his sinfulness. Then, and only then, when you felt quite without hope, could God reach down to you and open your heart to the joy of his forgiveness.

He used to ask people, 'How did you become a Christian?' and if their story did not contain the necessary amount of sulphur and brimstone he'd say to his wife afterwards, 'He's not really a Christian, you know.'

Apart from prayers after breakfast, Mr Smith put his children through prayers every night, only these were more exacting. After the evening meal Dad would get out the family Bible once again and read a passage of Scripture, after which the children in turn would have to repeat what they had learnt from it. The trick with this particular ordeal was to latch on to one phrase in the reading and repeat it over and over to yourself so that you didn't forget it: '. . . and Mary saw an angel . . . and Mary saw an angel . . . and Mary saw an angel . . .' This you could then trot out when your own time for cross-examination came around.

By the time he was 12 or so, Nico's attitude to religion was that he didn't want anything to do with it – though this determination was tinged with an uneasy feeling that he just might end up in hell.

Nevertheless, when he was still a young boy, Nico had a rather extraordinary experience.

Although their father was patriarchal, and in many ways distant and undemonstrative, the children worshipped him, often, when they were older, discussing the possibility of erecting a statue to his memory. One night, when he was about 9, Nico woke up quite suddenly and completely. It was just as if he'd woken up in the morning. He was wide awake and aware of his surroundings. There in the bedroom with him stood on old man. He had a white robe and he looked at Nico and smiled so lovingly.

And Nico thought, 'That can't be my father, looking so

lovingly at me.' And he called out, 'Daddy, Daddy.'

As he called, the figure disappeared, but a few moments later his father came into the room.

'What is it, Nico? Are you all right?'

'Yes, Dad, but I thought you were in the room with me.'

'No, son. You must have been dreaming. Go back to sleep.'

A few nights later it happened again. The same old man came, and he had a staff in his hand. As Nico lay there, wide awake, the old man bent over him.

'He had a wonderful deep look in his eyes and he smiled. I wasn't afraid to find this figure in the room. I thought it must be my father, but what puzzled me was that the look on his face could be so different. So loving. I called out again, "Daddy, Daddy".' Once again the figure disappeared and Nico's father came in.

The next morning Nico told his father exactly what had happened, and Mr Smith reassured him that it was just a dream. But Nico didn't think so. He thought then, and he thinks now, that it was God himself who came, because of the look in his eyes.

'I still don't know how to interpret it. Obviously God isn't a little old man, but maybe that was just a concept a young boy could understand. Perhaps at that stage it was just God's mercy to me, just to make me aware that somebody deeply loved me. A feeling that I was accepted.'

Despite the family's inability to express their love for one another in a physical way, the children at least had a real affection for each other. The girls were great friends with the boys, aiding and abetting them in all their misdoings. Nico's time for disappearing was in the evenings, when he'd go and catch donkeys to race in the bush. Jacobus used to disappear at night and ride the horses, threatening his little sisters with death if they ever said a word.

One night he came back with a broken arm – he'd been scrumping apples from a neighbour's tree. He didn't dare tell his parents about it and it was two or three days before they realised something was wrong. He got a hiding for that, but he also got taken to hospital – a fairly rare occurrence since neither of the parents believed in medicine and if anyone was ill, Dad would lay hands on them and pray. He had a real gift of healing.

There was, however, a certain medicine that Mother had a terrible weakness for. Vit Dulcis. Vit Dulcis was an inexplicable powder that came in a little tin box and was allegedly an old Dutch remedy for people who had fainting fits and weak hearts, and over the years Mrs Smith had perfected her fainting fits to a very fine art.

They used to come on when she'd had enough, usually after one of her brood had done something wrong. Having threatened the offender with God, she would then say, 'Just wait till your father comes home.' They would all wait until Father got home, the kids first having got the little tin box of Lennon's Vit Dulcis out in readiness for what was to come.

When Father arrived, Mother would explain the wickedness, ending with the words, 'I think I'm going to burst an artery,' with which, and with great grace, she would fall into an elegant collapse and faint away.

At first the children were very frightened when she did this, really believing that she would burst an artery, whatever an artery was (it sounded very serious) and that she had really fainted. But after many years of fainting fits the youngest child, Sylvia, realised that if she pinched her mother's nose during a faint, her mother was bound to open both her mouth and her eyes. They never told their mother they knew she was faking, nor did their father even so much as hint that this might be so. Instead he would fuss around her, get her a cup of tea and a little drop of the medicine on a sugar lump.

She always recovered very quickly and as they grew older the children felt this was the only way their mother could get the attention she craved from her undemonstrative husband.

They also began to see that their mother, in other circumstances, would have been a gay person. She loved to dance. They had an old wind-up gramophone, with a horn and His Master's Voice written on it, on which they would play 'Sugarbush I love you'. But their mother was never really given permission to enjoy herself because their father was so dour. He himself was quite unable to be free.

One of their abiding memories is of family picnics. Mother used to love picnics. She would prepare lovely food and go along with her fishing-rod and hang over the water – elegantly hang over the water, of course – while the children played. Father would sit some way off, under a tree, reading a book. A little later in life, when he was in his 50s, he allowed himself to take off his tie, and the shock of that reverberates around the family even now, forty-five years later. No one had ever seen Father's neck before.

But there was, perhaps, just one pleasure that all the family unequivocally enjoyed together, and that was their vintage car. It was one of those cars with a let-down seat at the back and a convertible roof. Unfortunately the roof was full of holes, but their mother got over this problem in the rainy season by sitting in the passenger seat underneath her umbrella.

The car had real leather upholstery, running-boards on either side and a tendency to break down.

One holiday time their parents went away and gave Jos, the eldest, then in her 20s, strict instructions not to drive it as the brakes had gone. But Jos had a boyfriend in Johannesburg whom she wanted to ring and the nearest phone was at the village shop.

They all piled into the car, Jos at the wheel and Nico on the running-board. His job was to jump off when they reached the gate, run to open it, close the gate behind them and then catch the car up and jump back on. What they had not bargained for were the cows. As they rounded the corner nearing the village they came across a small herd of cows somnambulent in the road.

All the kids started screaming, 'The cows, the cows,' and Nico jumped off and 'ran like hell', waving and yelling at the cows who viewed the steady approach of the Smith family car with nonchalant disdain. However, they lumbered to their feet just in time.

Luckily it was uphill from then on and the car was very heavy, so when they got to the village, Jos slowly turned it round and it ground to a stately halt. On the way home she drove it with great dignity into the hedge.

3

BLACK IS DIRTY

Nico was brought up to regard blacks as inferior and rather dirty. One of his earliest memories is of when he was about 4. He was outside in the backyard talking to old Maria, the washerwoman, when his mother called him in.

'Nico,' she said, 'there is something I must tell you. Never, never talk to a black person. The only time you talk to a black person is to give them a command.'

The black was, and is to many whites in South Africa today, not a person, but a function.

The Stallard Commission of 1922 put it quite frankly,

'It should be a recognised principle of government that natives – men, women and children – should only be permitted within municipal areas insofar and for so long as their presence is demanded by the wants of the white population . . . [they] should depart therefrom when they cease to minister to the needs of the white man.'

In Nico's childhood home the servants were treated tolerably provided they performed their functions adequately. When they no longer had a function, they were no longer wanted nor allowed. It was quite unthinkable to wonder where, or how they lived, or to enquire after their families or their health. The Smiths did make sure that their servants had enough to eat, and if they needed to go to hospital – then Mr Smith would take them. In this he was unusual. Most whites, then as now, didn't even know their servants' proper names.

Nico will tell you the story of the man who rang him up not long after he'd begun work in Mamelodi in 1982. What should he do? the man asked Nico. His gardener had just died and he didn't know what to do with the body.

'Has he got a wife?' asked Nico.

'I don't think so,' said the man.

'Well, then, you must get in touch with his relatives.'

'I don't know who his relatives are.'

'Where did he come from? Where did he go when he went home on leave?'

'I don't know.'

'What was his family name, that might help?'

'We always called him Johnnie.'

'How long was he working for you?' asked Nico.

'Forty years,' replied the man.

Mrs Smith also forbade the children to touch the tin mug and plate that the maids ate from. These were kept on a special shelf under the sink. One of the other children only had to say to her, 'Mu-um, Nico touched those things,' and Mother would immediately know what 'those things' were and Nico would be sent to go and wash his hands. Such was the common obsession about blacks and their cleanliness among the Afrikaners – an obsession which remains ingrained in many Afrikaans families today. It is still a struggle for many Afrikaners to let black people drink from their cups, and that is why the whole idea of sharing a meal with a black person is so difficult for them. Indeed, many years later, when Nico was in the mission field and attending an ecumenical conference, he found that he was psychologically unable to sit at a table with blacks and share a meal with them. He had to eat in a room all by himself – an event which, as it happens, was to trigger the revolution in his life.

Afrikaners will tell you now that one of the reasons their forebears were so anxious about cleanliness was because of the high incidence of TB among the Africans, but Nico has another theory, the root of which lies in a deep and primitive fear.

The most obvious cause of the fear is that the Africans are black, and in many early Western cultures the colour black was associated not only with what was dirty, but also with what was evil. In the fifth century, when the Christian monks were transcribing and illuminating the Bible, they depicted the devil as a little black figure. Nico believes that when Western people came into contact with blacks for the first time they had already been conditioned to think of them as in some way connected with darkness, with evil. Indeed the early Church in some parts of the world condoned slavery by arguing that since black people were 'of the devil' and all go to hell anyway, they could at least serve some useful purpose by being slaves to white Christians while they were on earth.

When the early settlers came to the Cape, slavery was already an accepted part of European culture, and from their first encounter with the blacks they would have seen them as subservient people and found it entirely fitting that they should be harnessed to the white man's needs. In fact it was commonly said at the time that 'nature had destined the blacks to be subservient for all time.' This negative attitude to blacks was reinforced by the differences they found in their culture, their appearance and their personal habits as well as the conflicts that arose over claims to the land and its wealth.

But there was another very basic fear that drove the Afrikaner into his racial laager, and finally to apartheid, and that was the fear of losing his identity, of being absorbed, of being overrun.

Nico was taught, as were all his generation and those before and since, that the white man landed at the Cape to find an empty land. The Voortrekker Monument, in Pretoria, depicts the struggles of the early Boers to free themselves from the British yoke and to carve out a land for themselves and their people. In the Hall of Heroes there is a huge marble frieze depicting the Afrikaner version of the Great Trek, and the text in the official guide reads:

It is nonsense to suppose that the interior of Southern Africa belonged to the Bantu and that the white man took it away from him. The Bantus penetrated from the north almost at the same time as the white man entered from the south. They had equal title to the country. The Voortrekkers wished to partition the country and live in peace because they had already experienced enough trouble in the Cape. But the Bantu were not amenable to reason. He respected only one thing and that was force.

David Harrison has described this as 'a comfortable view but unfortunately not quite true'. While the history of the early settlers is still unclear, it is generally established by non-nationalist historians that the Transvaal, where many of the Voortrekkers finally settled, was the home of the black people as early as the fifth century.

The blacks who live in South Africa today are thought to belong to a huge family of negroid tribes – over 70 million people – who live south of the equator. Between them they speak anything from 200–300 languages, referred to in general terms as 'Bantu'. Nobody is absolutely certain where they came from originally, but many anthropologists place their ancestors in the area around Lake Chad between what is now Nigeria and the Sudan, several centuries before the birth of Christ.

Portuguese sailors, shipwrecked on the Transkei coast in 1554, reported settlements of people 'very black in colour with woolly hair'. The land that the first settlers shared out among themselves after the first landing in 1652 had actually been the hunting-ground of the brown-skinned San people for centuries. Living alongside the San were the Khoikhoi, also brown skinned. It is reliably established that these two people had been trading with black men from farther north in cattle, iron, copper and cannabis long before the arrival of the white man.

But for men like Nico's father, South Africa was for the whites. Their understanding of history was, to put it crudely, that they'd got there first. When they finally encountered black men on their trek for freedom, in the north and east of the country, they were reluctant to admit that they had any prior claim to the lands.

Blacks were inferior and it was the duty of white colonisers to civilise and Christianise all those whom they considered to be barbarians. To this end they were within their rights not only to take the lands, but to take the blacks as well, as slaves and unpaid labour. And that's exactly what they did.

But behind all this racial arrogance there was a very real fear that Nico saw reflected in his father's eyes whenever he came back from Johannesburg or Pretoria and saw the great influx of blacks that had come looking for work – that was the fear of being overrun, of being absorbed, of losing an identity so desperately fought for, an identity God-given. In those very early days the Afrikaners felt most threatened by the British government and the indigenous people. Those who believed that the identity of the Afrikaner was God-given felt that mixing and 'equalisation' with the Africans would result in a loss of that identity. General De Wet put it like this: 'Providence has drawn the line between black and white and we must make that clear to the natives and not instil into their minds false ideas of equality.'

The concept of 'pure blood' was very dear to this new nation. The present National Party came to power in the 1940s on the basis of its race policy and in the first programme of principles of the National Party this was written:

'In our attitude towards the Natives the fundamental principle is the supremacy of the European population in a spirit of Christian trusteeship utterly rejecting every attempt to mix the races.'

Nico's aunt, on her death-bed in her 90s, epitomised this obsession when she lovingly stroked the back of his hand with hers and said, 'Remember, Nico, pure blood runs through these veins. Only pure blood.'

This concern for 'racial purity' found voice most dramatically in Hitler's Germany. At the Nazi Party congress in Nuremberg in 1935, Hermann Goering said, 'God created the races. He wanted no mixture. We therefore reject any attempt to adulterate this racial purity.' He was only reflecting the view voiced a few years earlier by Hitler in his book *Mein Kampf*: 'A people that fails to preserve the purity of its racial blood destroys the unity of the soul of the nation in all its manifestations. The most accursed of all crimes is cross-breeding. What we have to fight for is ... our race and nation ... and purity of its blood.'

The similarity between the Nazi régime in Germany and the present apartheid régime in South Africa is a recurring theme with Nico, and one that he comes back to time and again.

4

LOVE FOUND AND LOST

There were two emotional highlights in Nico's young life, and both occurred when he was 16. The first was his conversion to God, the second to women – well, one woman anyway, someone who was to give him a taste of what it meant to love and be loved, and whose memory he cherishes, even to this day.

The first happened in May 1945. A month before the Americans had dropped the atom bomb:

> That morning the teacher who taught us science came into the classroom and threw the newspaper on to the table and said; 'Children, from today we've entered a new era in the scientific world.' And he took a piece of chalk and turned around and made a small white dot in the middle of the blackboard and said; 'All the knowledge that we have up to now about the world is only represented by that little dot. And now we're going to enter this whole new area of a new world.'
>
> Science was my best subject and I was so excited by this I thought, now that is what I'm going to do. I'm going to become a teacher of science because I want to discover the big world around that small white dot.

It was to be a very short-lived desire.

Among the Afrikaner people it is accepted that in your last year at school you go to catechism class and finally join the Church. It is the socially acceptable thing to do.

So at 16, in his final year, Nico dutifully went along to the minister for two weeks with the other boys. They studied every day and took a test each afternoon. Being bright, Nico passed with flying colours and that was fine;

he was considered ready to be made a full member of the Church.

But it actually meant nothing to him at all. He didn't love God nor did he think God had any particular affection for him. Spiritually it was a non-event.

The day after his confirmation service he was walking down the street when he met a friend of his parents. Stopping to congratulate Nico, he said;

'Nico, by becoming a member of the Church you've become a good citizen of the country, a good member of the Afrikaner nation, but that doesn't necessarily mean you've become a member of God's people, of God's nation.'

Nico stopped short. What did he mean? And how did this man know that he didn't really belong to God?

For a whole month Nico struggled on his own. For the first time he realised that he wanted to belong to God, but he couldn't pray. He felt God was very far away from him, and that was frightening. He seemed to have no route to God, no way of contact. He tried to solve the difficulty intellectually, but got nowhere.

One Saturday lunch-time he found himself unable to eat. He pushed back his plate of food and hurriedly excusing himself from the table, went to the garage to get his bike. He rode off to the one man he felt he could really talk to. He knew that somehow he had to find peace of mind.

This man was an elderly minister who lived in the village. Nico asked him: how do you know you belong to God? How do you know you're a part of God's people?

The old man didn't use any arguments of his own, he just got down his Bible and read to Nico from the book of Isaiah:

He endured the suffering that should have been ours, the pain that we should have borne . . .
    Because of our sins he was wounded, beaten because of the evil we did. We are healed by the punishment he suffered, made whole by the blows he received.
    All of us were like sheep that were lost, each of us going his own way. But the Lord made the punishment fall on him, the punishment all of us deserved.

When he had finished reading, the old man said to Nico: 'I can't give you any other guarantee than that. I can only say what the Bible says; that Christ did it for you, that he took your punishment on himself so you needn't be afraid of punishment any more. If you believe that, and accept that Christ himself died for your sins, then you belong to God's people. There is no other guarantee.

And if the devil ever tries to tell you that it isn't true, that you are too sinful to belong to God, then turn to the Bible and read it again. It is all written there, inspired by God, and no one can ever take that truth from you.' Then he knelt down with Nico and prayed.

'I remember I was so overwhelmed by joy. I was just crying and crying, really touched by the Holy Spirit. And when I stood up I had that liberated feeling. I knew that I really belonged to God, that Christ had done it for me. It was wonderful.'

It was May 5th, 1945, and despite all the traumas of the years that were to follow, that inner peace and sense of belonging have never left him.

When he told his sister about his experience she wrote back immediately and said that if he had discovered such a wonderful truth, then he could help many other people in their struggle for faith by becoming a minister.

'When I read her letter I knew immediately that she was right, that I should become a minister. It seemed a very rational decision.'

It was not, however, so rational to Nico's father. Perhaps he didn't smell the necessary quantity of brimstone, it's hard to say, but he was very cautious about confirming that Nico had had a real conversion experience. 'Let's wait and see how it works out,' he said.

When Nico went on to explain that he felt a calling to the ministry, Mr Smith was even less impressed, pointing out that it was only four weeks since he had been convinced he should become a science teacher!

Well, Nico couldn't argue with that. If his father thought he was too young to make a decision, maybe he was. He accepted the challenge to spend two years in business with his brother before going any further. He

was, after all, only just 16, with his final year at school still
to complete.

*   *   *

It was in this final period at school that he fell in love with
one of the young teachers. She was only about three or four
years older than he and for some reason he never really
understood, developed a real affinity towards him.

'She used to invite me to come and visit her in her room
in the evenings. We would have long talks about everything under the sun, and she would let me embrace her! I
felt enormously wicked, but I really loved this woman. I
thought it was too wonderful that she could care for me
and treat me like a grown man and talk to me so freely. It
was pure heaven!'

What Nico didn't know was that his young teacher was
also having an affair with the English master. When he
left school Nico wrote a few letters to her, but never
received any answers. Until one day a letter did come:
'Nico, I'm so sorry. I should never have allowed you to
become so close to me. I'm going to be married . . .'

'For one moment it was as if the whole earth was
opening under me. And the next moment I can remember
that I said in my heart: so that is that. And I took the
letter and tore it into small pieces. And that was the
end.'

Although it was a hurt reaction, it was also a definite
decision. He was not going to mourn. He recognised that
that was the end. And they never made contact again.

Looking back, he doesn't think she behaved improperly
to him. 'She was a lovely woman. And she was almost holy
to me and just to touch her was something out of this
world. For some reason she did have a special feeling for
me, and it was lovely.'

Nico was not to touch another woman, or to fall in love
again, until he met Ellen Faul some six years later.

*   *   *

Even disobeying your father can be God-inspired, according to Nico. Well that's his interpretation of the events of

his life that led him, at the age of 16, to study theology at Pretoria University.

His father had said he must work for two years before making any further decisions, but work was hard to come by in those days and the only vacancy he could find was in Pretoria. The firm, mindful of his age, said they would only give Nico the job if he first found lodgings.

For a whole day he and his brother Boertjie walked the length of the city. Up one street, down another, knocking on the doors of every possible boarding-house or private home that looked as if it might have accommodation to spare.

At about 3 o'clock in the afternoon they knocked on the door of the Swan Villa in Proes Street. Yes, said the landlady, that very morning a young man had just moved out without giving any reason, and his place would be available, but Nico would have to share the room with two others.

It was a deal, and the next morning he started work. What he soon discovered was that his digs were only one block away from the university which took extramural students. Why should he wait two years 'just to see how I feel'? Why not enrol now? His father couldn't stop him.

So Nico enrolled for four subjects: Greek, Hebrew, Afrikaans and Sociology. He started work every morning at 8.30, knocked off at 4.30 and walked down to the university for the beginning of lectures at 5 o'clock. They continued until 11 when he went home and worked until midnight.

To his own surprise at the end of the first year he passed all four subjects, even though the lecturer had said it was impossible. Of the twenty-five extramural students who started the course with him, only five passed the end-of-year exams.

The second year was not so easy. There was even more study than before and he began to work later and later, not going to bed until 2am until he worked himself up into such a state that even when he went to bed, he was unable to sleep.

He began to suffer symptoms of anxiety and stress and

in the end his doctor told him he must get away until his body and mind had returned to a normal routine.

So he went, but he took his books with him, and came back to pass all four subjects once again. Of the five students that had survived the first year, only Nico and one other survived the second.

Now even his father could not doubt either his ability or his determination to study for the ministry and, finding the money for his son's studies, he at last allowed Nico to become a full-time student.

5

FRIENDS AND BROTHERS

Looking at you with his huge brown, hound dog eyes, Nico says: 'You know, I sometimes think I was born with an inferiority complex. I've always felt that I can't do things. Although I went through university so young, I always believed that I just couldn't do it.

'Even now sometimes when I am asked to speak I go through a trauma of fear and suffering. There are times when I say: "God, I can't continue. I am going to resign as a minister of your word and get a job where I never have to speak in public." Those times are hell. They come so unexpectedly. It's like the devil hitting me in the face.

'I suppose it must spring from my father, because he was such a perfectionist and expected so much, and from my mother, and from this and from that. But understanding is not releasing me from the reality!

'Ellen and I have just had to accept together that it is part of my being, and I have to live with it.' But even as a young student it got so bad that Nico eventually visited the university psychologist and asked him if he was abnormal, if he was going mad. He was under psychoanalysis for some time, but nothing was ever made clear.

But that inner anxiety is not what his friends know or remember about Nico during his early years. They recall his humour and vitality, his innate joy of life.

Charles Fensham, who knew him from boyhood, remembers the time Nico spent a whole day handcuffed to a friend. 'Nico had such a twinkle in those days. He had an inside inspiration, a drive. He was a good person to be with, and very much loved.'

But, even so, there was something hidden, something he

was keeping back. 'I think it was his belief,' says Fensham. 'He was not certain how to express it and it was easier for him to have a joke than to reveal his more serious side. Later on he changed completely. Today he seems a different person.'

Nico's two greatest friends at that time – and for many years to come – were Murray Jansön and Carel Boshoff. With Murray he shared many cultural interests. He was a very sensitive and fastidious young man with a deep empathy for other human beings – provided they were white, of course. Many people would go to Murray with their problems, and he was later to become a gifted psychologist as well as a fine preacher.

Carel Boshoff was infused with a great evangelistic zeal. He and Nico would go down-town on a Saturday morning and distribute pamphlets and sell Bibles to the blacks. Speaking for himself, Nico would say that this zeal sprang not so much from any feeling of love for the blacks, as from a sense of 'Christian duty to convert the heathen'.

All three friends were staunch Nationalists. All three were to become professors. All three were to join the powerful and exclusive Afrikaner Broederbond. Carel Boshoff went on to become chairman of the Broederbond until he resigned because he felt it was becoming too liberal.

Years later, when Nico's views on Afrikaner nationalism so dramatically changed, he was to feel much as the German martyr Bonhoeffer did when he wrote to Karl Barth: 'I feel that in some way I don't understand I have got up against all my friends. My views about what should be done have seemed to cut me off from them more and more . . .'

Certainly Carel Boshoff was one day to walk out of Nico's study and end nearly twenty-five years of friendship, accusing him of being a 'Cape Liberal' (a high term of abuse in Afrikanerdom) and a traitor to his people. Nico has often wanted to make it up with Boshoff, but he can't face Carel's wife – the daughter of Hendrik Verwoerd is a formidable lady!

Murray Jansön and Nico are still friends, still talk of each other with affection and love, yet both, in their private moments, feel a deepening gulf between them, a lack of understanding on the part of the other, a real sorrow at a separation they can hardly bring themselves to admit. But before things got this bad, one of the organisations that bound the three friends together was the Afrikaner Broederbond – the Brotherhood.

It is not possible to understand the true power structure of South Africa, or the events in Nico Smith's life, without understanding the role and workings of this powerful underground movement.

The nearest thing to the Broederbond in Europe would be the Freemasons, but the power of the Brotherhood is even deeper and more insidious. It is the Broederbond who originally formulated apartheid, and who have – in secret, and unknown to the rest of South African society – initiated, developed and controlled most of the policies of the National Party over the last forty years.

Although the Bond was finally exposed by journalists Ivor Wilkins and Hans Strydom in 1978, its power is largely undiminished. In their book, *The Super-Afrikaners*, they write:

Although it has only 12,000 scrupulously selected members, it plots and influences the destiny of all 25 million South Africans, black and white. By stealth and sophisticated political intrigues, this 60-year-old organisation has waged a remarkable campaign to harness political, social and economic forces in South Africa to its cause of ultimate Afrikaner domination . . .

The South African Government today is the Broederbond and the Broederbond is the Government. No Afrikaner government can rule South Africa without the support of the Broederbond. No Nationalist Afrikaner can become Prime Minister unless he comes from the organisation's select ranks.

They point out that not only is P. W. Botha a member, but so were his four predecessors: Malan, Strijdom, Verwoerd and Vorster. And in 1978 every member except two of the Cabinet were also in the Broederbond.

The policies of the Broederbond – with its exclusive membership of pure Afrikaners (no English speakers are allowed) – reach into every section of the nation's political and professional life, and to cross the Afrikaner Broederbond – especially if you have once been a member – is to invite trouble. Yet its beginnings seemed harmless enough.

On June 5th, 1918, fourteen men met at 32 Marathon Street, Johannesburg, the private home of Danie du Plessis. They were discussing the plight of the Afrikaner people, at that time still very poor and struggling to retain their dignity and identity under British rule. This group of friends felt there was a need to form an organisation 'in which Afrikaners could find each other in the midst of great confusion and disunity, and be able to work together for the survival of the Afrikaner people in South Africa and the promotion of its interests.'

The official history of the Bond says: 'This is how the Afrikaner Broederbond originated, out of an urgent need of a people standing on the threshold of permanent extinction.'

And so the Afrikaner Broederbond was formed. Its first functions were purely cultural. They organised lectures, dinner-parties and picnics. They started a library with cheap subscriptions for members. They held celebrations to mark the significant events in their history. They held classes in Dutch and ran book competitions. Their whole aim was to unite the Afrikaner people and build up a sense of their history, culture and identity. And in this they were extremely successful.

Membership was not originally secret. The Broederbond had their own lapel-badge and tie-clips, their own handshake, their own song and their own flag. As an organisation it played a vital role in helping a demoralised people to regain their rightful dignity.

David Harrison writes:

But within three years, the bloom of early innocence had faded. On August 26th, 1921 the . . . members voted to turn the Broederbond into a secret organisation. Members, particularly civil servants and teachers, claimed they were persecuted because of their open association with the Bond. One member, recalling that meeting years later, said it was 'a matter of tactics and self-preservation'.

These were the days when the Afrikaner was still the butt of English racialism and ridicule.

Soon absolute secrecy was the rule. Broeders were instructed not even to tell their wives that they were members. They were under oath not to reveal anything that took place at the meetings, or to address one another openly as brothers. They met mostly after dark in private homes, and the host brother was encouraged to make sure that his wife and family were out for the evening and the servant given the night off.

Although they continued to claim to be a cultural organisation, their aims quickly developed into a determination to achieve Afrikaner domination over the whole of South Africa. Their stated desire was political control of the country, and in their daily business and transactions they were sworn to promote the interest of the Afrikaner over and above any other member of the community.

The Bond is run on a cell system, very like the Communist Party cell structure, with members of each small branch, or cell, being known only to one another and the executive council. When the Bond first started, in 1918, there was one cell with thirty-seven members. By 1930 there were twenty-three cells with five hundred members. Today there are some eight hundred cells with twelve thousand members. All these members are in the professions, or in positions of social significance.

Only one man ever tried to break the Broederbond before it became too powerful, and that was the then Prime Minister, General J. B. M. Hertzog, in 1935. He accused the Bond of creating dissension among the people and of inciting one race against another 'in irreconcilable aversion'.

In his famous Smithfield speech that year he said: 'Has

the Afrikaner nation sunk to so hopeless a level that it must seek its salvation in a secret conspiracy for the advancement of race hatred ... ? Is there no higher aspiration for the sons and daughters of South Africa, no nobler task, than that of racial strife and dissension? Is there no higher ideal for our children to attain than that of racial domination ... ?'

General Hertzog, one-time hero of the Afrikaner people, the veteran Boer campaigner and an architect of guerrilla tactics, was to die a lonely and rejected man, the victim of a smear campaign engineered in vengeance by the Broederbond. No politician ever took on the Broederbond in public again.

6

HOW THE DUTCH REFORMED CHURCH ADOPTED APARTHEID

As a student Nico was fascinated by the concept of a pure race. His interest was fanned by the leading professor at the seminary, Jeff Cronje, who, as it happens, was the first man ever to coin the term 'apartheid' as a political concept in a book he published in 1942.

There were two main streams of thought that led to the formulation and adoption of apartheid by the Dutch Reformed Church (DRC, known in Afrikaans as the NGK, the Nederduitse Gereformeerde Kerk). The first came from the Free University of Amsterdam where many Dutch Reformed ministers went to do their doctoral studies. There they came under the influence of the Dutch theologian, Abraham Kuyper. Kuyper talked about the 'pluriformity of creation' – that God had created everything in variety in order to express the richness of his creation. Kuyper never had separation of peoples in mind, but his ideas were manipulated by theologians in South Africa who argued that they had a responsibility, therefore, to protect the richness of God's creation by maintaining the identities of different peoples. Not to do so would dishonour God.

In a book of collected essays, edited by Cronje, Professor E. P. Groenewald, who was the leading theologian at the Pretoria faculty of theology, put forward the argument that because God chose Israel as a special people that was evidence that God wanted apartheid ('separateness'). And he wanted it to be total, which meant absolutely no mixing of the races. To support his argument he cited passages of

Scripture which have been used ever since by those trying to prove the point:

> Deuteronomy 32:8: 'The Most High assigned nations their lands; he determined where peoples should live.'
>
> Acts 17:26: 'From one man he created all races of mankind and made them live throughout the whole earth. He himself fixed beforehand the exact times and the limits of the places where they would live.'

Groenewald also used the story of the Tower of Babel from Genesis 11 to support his arguments. Sinful man, he said, tried to go against the will of God, which is separateness (apartheid) by creating unity and homogeneity of the human race. God toppled the plan by causing confusion among the builders of the tower so that they ended up speaking different languages and could no longer understand one another. He then divided the nations and distributed them all over the world.

However obscure these arguments may seem, they became generally accepted by the DRC. It must be remembered that the Church was deeply involved with the Afrikaner struggle for a national identity. It sympathised with the Boer vision that they were a chosen people, and with their need for political and economic independence. Many Dutch Reformed ministers became members of the Broederbond.

Their beliefs are perhaps most simply and succinctly expressed in a document published by the Mission Council of the DRC.

> ... God divided humanity into races, languages and nations. Differences are not only willed by God, but are perpetuated by him. Equality between natives, coloured and Europeans includes a misappreciation of the fact that God, in his providence, made people into different races and nations ...
>
> Far from the word of God encouraging equality, it is an established Scriptural principle that in every community ordination there is a fixed relationship between authorities ... those who are culturally and spiritually

advanced have a mission to leadership and protection of the less advanced ... The natives must be led and formed towards independence so that eventually they will be equal to the Europeans, but each on their own territory and each serving God and their own fatherland.

Father Trevor Huddleston, that 'turbulent priest' from the Community of the Resurrection, who has been a thorn in the flesh of the present régime for the last forty years or more, describes this theology as 'sub-Christian'.

It carries with it the implication that all racial differences are not only willed by God in his act of creation, but are to be sustained by him to the end of time. It further involves the assumption that there has been no intermingling of races through the centuries without loss, and presumably sin – since such intermingling must be, ipso facto, contrary to the Divine Will. And it makes no reference to his Son.

In other words the view expressed here ... is sub-Christian. I say sub-Christian rather than 'Old Testament' because I suppose that somewhere behind the obscure and murky twilight theology it represents there are remembrances of the gospel message. I cannot find them.

The truth is that the Calvinistic doctrines upon which the faith of the Afrikaner is nourished contain within themselves ... exaggerations so distorting and so powerful that it is very hard indeed to recognise the Christian faith they are supposed to enshrine. Here, in this fantastic notion of the immutability of race, is present in different form the predestination idea; the concept of an elect people of God.

The real problem with the DRC, as Huddleston sees it, is that it cannot conceive of a relationship between black and white in this world, which is in any way real or tangible in terms of love.

*   *   *

But the Church has not always been racist. At the end of the eighteenth century, when it was the official church of the colony, it experienced an awareness of its responsibility to do missionary work, and because of a sincere desire to spread the message of the Christian Gospel, growing numbers of slaves and indigenous people became converted and joined the congregations of the Church.

And that's when the trouble started. Until 1824 the DRC was still part of the church in Holland from which it took its authority. But the moment it became independent a group within the Church appealed for separated churches for black and white. This was dismissed by the new synod who said that such a thing could not happen under any circumstances. It was quite contrary to Bible teaching. It went so far as to say that the sharing of Holy Communion by the different races in the same church must be seen as an 'immutable rule founded in the infallible word of God'.

But the segregationists worried away and worried away, and as more and more blacks joined the congregations, opposition to worshipping with them grew among the whites.

And so, pressured by the ground swell of opinion, the synod of the DRC reluctantly agreed in 1857 that there should be separate church buildings. They in no way tried to justify the move theologically, and were clearly uncomfortable about the decision. What they actually said was that it was 'desirable and scriptural that our members converted from the heathen should be taken up and incorporated into our existing congregations wherever possible', but that separate buildings should also be provided when 'the weakness of some' made it necessary.

All this happened at a time when the flames of racism and nationalism were being fanned into a roaring fire by the imperialistic demands of the British, and the Boers, in desperation, were beginning to organise their escape.

They set off on their Great Trek north and formed two republics, one in the Transvaal and the other in the Orange Free State, writing into the constitutions of both that there should be no equality between black and white in either state or church.

By the end of the 1930s the fragile relationship between the Dutch and English-speaking churches finally broke down when the DRC left the Christian Council of South Africa. The stated aims of the Council had been to promote inter-church and inter-racial co-operation, but British insistence on the equality of blacks once again proved too much for the DRC. In giving reasons for their withdrawal, William Nicol, a Dutch Reformed minister and Chairman of the Council, said:

> The last reason for the failure was the deepest of all: our conflicting views on the right relations between white and black. The English-speaking missionary, especially the one born overseas, wishes to see as little difference as possible between the white man and the native. He does not hesitate to welcome the civilised native to his dining-table, in many cases the native finds lodging for the night as an honoured guest among such white people. For us, on the other hand, the thought that we should use the same bathrooms and bathroom conveniences as even the most highly civilised native, is revolting. These principles run through all our conduct.

And so eighty years after the Church had made its first hesitant concession to 'the weakness of some', it finally gave apartheid – with the help of men like Professor Groenewald – its theological stamp of approval.

Because the Church was so deeply committed to the liberation of the Afrikaner people it became inextricably involved in the National Party and went on to give its wholehearted support to the acts of parliament that legalised racialism and oppression.

*   *   *

The other mainstream of thought that led to the formulation of apartheid came from Germany where the young Afrikaner intellectuals of the 1930s were sent to study.

There they came under the influence of German romanticism which believed in the superiority of certain peoples.

Professor Cronje, who had a profound influence on the sociology students of Nico's era, had himself studied in Germany and been deeply affected by the German Romantic Movement. While he never openly supported the Nazis, as most of the leading intellectuals of the time appeared to do, it was clear to Nico from his books that he had a deep sympathy for them. Indeed there was widespread sympathy for the Third Reich among most Afrikaners who were also very anti-Semitic, fearing that because of their considerable business acumen, the Jews were in a position to exploit the Afrikaner and become rich at his expense. The Afrikaners at this time still had very little economic clout.

Nico believes that had the number of Jews in South Africa been larger at that time, and had the Afrikaners not been hamstrung by the British legal system, they might well have gone as far as the Germans in wanting to eradicate the Jews systematically.

Afrikaans politicians and intellectuals were quite open in their support of the Fascists and Nazis. They used the same political language and phraseology and, when they eventually came to power in 1948, brought into being a series of laws that paralleled those of the Third Reich to a quite extraordinary degree, and systematically reduced the black – socially, professionally and economically – to the status of a non-person. As Dr Sipo Mzimela put it; 'They embarked on a programme of legislation designed to translate into reality their theory that blacks were subhuman.'

Leading churchmen quoted Nazi propaganda from their pulpits. In 1940, J. D. Vorster, who was later to become an important figure in the DRC, told his congregation; 'Hitler's *Mein Kampf* shows the way to greatness – the path of South Africa. Hitler gave the Germans a calling. He gave them a fanaticism which causes them to stand back for no one. We must follow his example because only by such a holy fanaticism can the Afrikaner nation achieve its calling.'

This, then, was the intellectual climate in which the young Nico was nurtured and for his final-year diploma he wrote on the concept of self-love and mixed marriage. The only problem was that his arguments came 'a bit unstuck. I tried to argue that since Jesus commanded us to love our neighbour as ourselves, we had in effect a command there to love ourselves. How then could I, obeying this command, enter into a mixed marriage which would mean mixing the blood of those born from such a marriage. I have to respect myself as God created me, and it would be against God's will to mix blood, through marriage, which would endanger the separateness in which we had been created.

'The trouble was I came to the conclusion that the Bible did not command you to love yourself. That in fact what Jesus was saying was, since human beings, in their weakness, do love themselves, they must apply the same strong, self-interested love to their neighbour. If you like, turn the weakness of self-love into the strength of selfless love.

'The professor didn't like this at all. He was very disappointed and gave me a low mark! But while I felt I couldn't use this particular argument to support apartheid in marriage, I didn't change my mind about apartheid. I still believed it right. I still believed that God wanted people to maintain their different identities, and I still believed that the Afrikaners were God's elect, and I, therefore, was one of his chosen people.'

7

SOUTH AFRICA'S THIRD REICH

Hundreds of students were roaring up and down Church Street – the longest street in southern Africa – waving their arms and shouting out their freedom songs for the whole city to hear:

> Do you hear the mighty thunder
> As it rolls across the plains.
> It's the song of a people awakening
> And it causes hearts to tremble . . .

On and on they ran, Nico among them, looping in and out of the trees and lamp posts that still bore the party posters:

Vote for the National Party. Support apartheid – the only solution.

Vote for apartheid. Make sure your children stay white.

Vote National Party. Keep the country white.

And they had, they had. The unbelievable, hardly dared to be hoped for, had happened. Old man Smuts had been outvoted. The Afrikaners had won the election. Their own party, flesh of their flesh, bone of their bone, nurtured in secret by the Broederbond, supported in public by the DRC, had won the general election. They were free at last. Free from the British. Their own people with their own country. It was a heady day.

For Nico and his friends it hadn't been a total surprise. Two hours before the results had been announced, one of the students in his hostel came hurtling along on his bicycle. Breathless from the exertion, he told Nico and the others that he'd just come from the barber's. As he was having his hair cut, who should walk in but General Smuts, looking as if he was ready to die.

'That can only mean one thing. I'm sure the old man's lost.'

Sure enough, a couple of hours later the results were announced and Smuts, then 79, had even lost his own seat in Standerton to Wentzel du Plessis, a staunch Broeder-bonder.

The new prime minister, Dr D. F. Malan, a founder member of the Broederbond, was jubilant. 'Today,' he said, 'South Africa belongs to us once more. For the first time since Union, South Africa is our own. May God grant that it will always remain so.'

Journalist David Harrison reports that Colin Legum, then general secretary of the Labour Party, met a lift attendant who put it more bluntly. 'From now on,' he said, 'a kaffir is a kaffir again.'

*   *   *

The policies of apartheid that the National Party (known as the Nats) began almost immediately to implement, had already been forged in secrecy by the Broederbond – a fact of which the general public were quite unaware. But the idea of separate development, now made respectable by the electorate's vote, rapidly took legal shape and form, and the similarities between Nazi Germany and the newly emerging Afrikaner South Africa were startling.

The Nazis also acted from the belief that they were a chosen people ordained by God for a special purpose. They were the '*Herrenrasse*', the master race. Hitler appealed to the Germans to carry out 'the mission appointed for them by the Creator of the Universe'.

The Nazi Party programme of 1920 made it clear that the two most important ingredients of Nazism (they called it National Socialism) were nationalism and racism – in this case anti-Semitism. The Jews were singled out as a race unfit to be German citizens because they did not have 'pure blood'. What the Nazis were working towards was the elimination of everything Jewish. They wanted a country free from Jews and the German *Volk* free from Jewish blood.

To this end they introduced a series of laws which affected every aspect of Jewish life, and these the National Party of South Africa imitated, almost law by law, only stopping short of final mass extermination.

There had been clear signs of co-operation between the Nats and the Nazis in the thirties and early forties. Hendrik Verwoerd, later to become prime minister and known as the 'architect of apartheid', was at this time editor of the leading Afrikaans paper *Die Transvaler*. His editorials strongly and openly supported the Nazis.

Addressing a rally of Afrikaner supporters in 1942, John Vorster, also destined to become a prime minister, spelled it out very clearly, 'We stand for Christian Nationalism which is an ally of National Socialism. You can call this antidemocratic principle dictatorship if you wish. In Italy it is called Fascism, in Germany National Socialism, and in South Africa, Christian Nationalism.'

Dr Malan, before he won the election of 1948, told his voters: 'Perhaps eighty to eighty-five per cent of National Socialism has been taken up in the National Party programme, which the Party will carry out in letter and in spirit when it comes to power.'

And this they did.

But it's only fair to say that while the Nats moved with lightning speed through a series of legislation designed, as David Harrison put it, 'to enforce separation in every sphere of life, from buses to bed', legislated racial discrimination had begun years before under British rule.

The South Africa Act, passed in 1909, removed the right of blacks to sit in parliament. And later they were deprived of their common-role franchise. The Natives Land Act of 1913 set aside certain areas of the country as native reserves. Other laws passed in the 1920s established segregated black areas in the cities, controlled the number of blacks allowed to work in urban areas and allowed their removal if they were 'surplus to requirements'. The governor-general could also introduce curfew measures, and so on.

But that was nothing, compared with what was to come. It took the National Party to implement, 'in letter and in spirit' the laws they had first seen and so much admired in the Third Reich.

The first thing a country has to do, if basing a law on racial discrimination, is to determine what race individuals belong to. This proved, for both the Nazis and the Nats, easier said than done.

The German Walther Hofer comments:

> How difficult it was . . . to determine clearly this racial membership, is clear from the further regulations that a grandparent would unquestionably qualify as a full Jew if he was a member of the Jewish faith. Well, what an intellectual criterion to determine the so-called biologically definitive racial membership . . . No wonder that a man like Goering could say: I decide who is a Jew!

The South Africans also had problems. In 1950 they passed the Population Registration Act which set out the guidelines for deciding a person's race. A coloured person was one 'who is not a white person or a native'; a native was 'in fact, or is generally accepted as, a member of any aboriginal race or tribe of Africa', and a white person was one who 'in appearance obviously is, or is generally accepted as, a white person, but does not include a person who, although in appearance obviously a white person, is generally accepted as a coloured person.'

The task was clearly ludicrous. Officials appointed to carry out classifications in those early days resorted to what became known as the 'pencil in the hair' technique. If a pencil pushed into the hair of the person stayed there because the hair was crinkly, then he was put down as 'African'. If it fell out because the hair was straighter, then he was 'coloured'.

David Harrison writes:

Families found themselves inexplicably divided. Couples of different race groups, who had married before such unions were declared illegal, could find their children assigned indiscriminately to one or other group. Parents classified black could be told their children were coloured and must therefore live in a separate area. It was not unknown for brothers and sisters of the same parents to be given different classifications.

'Classification' is still going on. Between July 1982 and June 1983 a total of 462 coloured people became white; four whites became coloured, seventy-one Africans became coloured, eleven coloureds became African, thirty-seven coloureds became Indian, eight coloureds became Chinese, nine Chinese became white, four whites became Chinese, three whites became Indian, two Malay became white, fifteen Indian became Malay, two Africans became Indian, and another two Africans became Griqua. Two Indians became 'other Asian', and so did one African. In all 690 human beings were reclassified.

If you live in South Africa, your racial classification affects every area of your life.

The first Act the Nats passed was the Prohibition of Mixed Marriages Act followed closely by the Immorality Amendment Act. The first forbade marriage between whites and non-whites, and said that any such marriage entered into outside South Africa was also void. In other words, you might be legally married in the eyes of say, Ghanaian law, but as far as South Africa was concerned, you were living 'in sin'. Which meant that you were contravening the Immorality Amendment Act forbidding sexual intercourse between black and white. Maximum penalty if found guilty: seven years' imprisonment with hard labour.

The anguish this Act induced resulted in broken homes, social disgrace, mental breakdown and suicide. It was modelled on the Nazi marriage and immorality laws which prohibited marriages between Germans and Jews and which also had a clause stating that marriages conducted outside the country would be considered void. They went a step further and encouraged divorce among couples with a mixed background. The penalty for sleeping with a Jew was imprisonment for the German, for the Jew it was death.

Property rights in Nazi Germany and in South Africa

Decree of Acquiring Jewish Property, December 1938: Article II

'A Jew can be required to sell, within a given period of time, his farm, forest, other property connected with his farm and forest, his real estate or other property, either together or separately.'

A further clause added that no Jew could purchase real estate, and a year later a further law was passed making it possible forcibly to remove Jews from the homes they owned, and put them all together in 'Jewish Houses'. A day earlier it had been announced that Jews would not be eligible for rent subsidies.

The Nats approached the problem by passing the Group Areas Act, regarded as the cornerstone of apartheid. Its purpose was to keep blacks, Indians and coloureds out of white residential areas. To this end the country was carved up in such a way that every section of the population was given a different residential area. The Act rode roughshod over traditional property rights, forcibly evicted thousands of blacks, coloureds and Indians from their homes, dumping them in designated areas which frequently had few or no amenities and were often miles away from their places of work. Businesses were destroyed, many families having to start again from scratch in areas where there were no facilities or resources of any kind.

The Act also took away the freehold rights of blacks, and urban blacks were made to live in designated areas known as 'locations'. They were not allowed to own their property, they had no security of tenure and were forbidden to do anything to improve the squalid quality of their homes. The thinking behind this was to make life so uncomfortable that they would voluntarily return 'home' to their appointed 'homelands'.

The Act also empowered the Minister of Native Affairs to order the demolition of a location and move all the blacks to another site without consulting them, whenever the government felt it necessary.

Citizenship laws in Nazi Germany and South Africa

The Citizenship Law passed at the Congress in Nuremberg said;

A Reich citizen is a national of German or kindred blood only, one who through his conduct proves that he is willing and suitable to serve the German Volk and Reich faithfully . . .

Only those who are fellow Germans shall be citizens of our State. Only those who are of German blood can be considered as our fellow citizens.

Those who are not citizens of the state must live in Germany as foreigners, and must be subject to the law of aliens.

The Jews had become stateless overnight.

In 1950 the Minister of Native Affairs assured the white electorate that blacks would have 'no political or social or other rights equal with Europeans', and in 1959 the Promotion of Bantu Self-Government Act was passed which finalised the process of disenfranchisement started by the British. All rights of South African citizenship were finally taken from the blacks.

'The National Party policy,' said Johannes Strijdom, later prime minister, 'is division and apartheid. The native is to live his own life in his own area. The native must only be allowed to leave his area to come to work in the European areas as a temporary worker. His wife and children must remain behind.'

The Nazi and National Party Education Laws

When the Nazi party came to power in 1933 Jewish and German children went to the same schools, except in the case of Confessional schools which were run on religious lines. The Nazis immediately put an end to this social integration by at first limiting the number of Jewish children allowed in German schools, and then by expelling them altogether. Jews had to have their own schools.

The mission schools in South Africa, which were responsible for most black education and all black teacher-training, were accused by many whites of feeding dangerous 'liberal' ideas into untrained minds. *The Forum* wrote in 1953 that the 'academically educated non-European, with no roots in reality and his head full of book learning' could be 'a social misfit and a political danger'.

The Bantu Education Act of 1953 put the control of all black education in the hands of central government and economically undermined the mission schools, many having to close as a result. The effect of this was a lowering of educational standards and the deliberate stated aim of the government was to supply a different (and intellectually inferior) education for blacks.

When the Minister of Native Affairs, Hendrik Verwoerd, introduced the Bill in parliament, the Prime Minister, Daniel Malan, explained why they felt blacks had to receive a separate and inferior education:

> For a white minority to face a large majority of civilised and educated non-whites wishing to share our way of life, and striving for equality in all respects [would make] the fight for a White South Africa immeasurably more difficult.

In the debate that followed, Verwoerd put his case:

> The school must equip the Bantu to meet the demands which the economic life of South Africa will impose on him ... There is no place for him in the European community above the level of certain forms of labour. Within his own community, however, all doors are open ... Until now he has been subject to a school system which drew him away from his own community and misled him by showing him the green pastures of European society in which he is not allowed to graze ... What is the use of teaching a Bantu child mathematics when it cannot use it in practice? ... That is absurd. Education must train and teach people in accordance with their opportunities in life ... It is therefore necessary that native education should be controlled in such a way

that it should be in accordance with the policy of the State.

Employment Laws in Nazi Germany and South Africa

In 1933 the Jews were expelled from the civil service. Five years later they were forbidden to work in a wide range of commercial activity which had the result of removing Jewish participation from large sections of German commerce, industry and the professions. Even doctors had their licences withdrawn and were allowed to treat only fellow Jews.

The Industrial Conciliation Act, No 28, of 1956, inhibited blacks from a whole range of work in commerce and industry, relegating them to the most menial tasks. They were forbidden to hold senior positions or to supervise whites.

One of the implications of this Act was felt in the medical profession where black doctors were unable to treat their own patients in provincial hospitals if this meant their being in a position of authority over a white nurse. It also meant that they were prevented from accepting senior specialist posts in the hospitals serving black communities if this meant their being in a position of authority over junior white doctors or students. Nor were they allowed to treat white patients.

Collective bargaining and Wages

Unemployed Jews could be forced to work on construction and reclamation projects, and sent wherever the German labour offices decided. They were separated from other labourers and no concessions were made for invalids, or distinctions drawn between the type of work suitable for young people and adults, and they were paid for 'actual work done'. Their earnings were drastically reduced and fringe benefits removed from their pay. One commentator wrote that 'Industry had been given the right to almost unlimited exploitation: to pay minimum wages for maximum work.'

Since the whites considered that they would be committing 'race suicide' if they gave the blacks any 'political weapons', The Native Labour (Settlement of Disputes) Act of 1953 forbade blacks to form trade unions. A subsequent Act disbarred them from the means of collective bargaining on the grounds that this could only be done through the trade unions. Without the protection afforded workers by the trade union, the employers could pay black workers whatever they wished. The Ministry of Labour said the principle of equal pay for equal work applied to whites only. Many blacks had to survive on subsistence wages.

The courts were then, in 1970, given the power to 'remove' blacks from urban areas to work on farms, institutions or rehabilitation schemes where they would have to stay for as long as the government deemed it necessary. According to General Circular Number 25, 'The aged, the unfit, widows, women with dependent children [will be] normally regarded as non-productive and as such have to be resettled in the homelands.'

Identification documents

Just before the outbreak of the Second World War, Jews over the age of 15 were compelled to carry identification documents. 'Failure to comply . . . will be treated as an exceptionally serious offence.'

In 1957 the Nationalists passed their own law – one of the notorious 'pass laws' – which also compelled blacks of 16 and over to carry an identification document known as the reference book, or pass-book. 'Any native who fails to produce the Reference Book on demand shall be guilty of an offence and liable to the penalties prescribed.'

The 'penalties prescribed' included heavy fines, imprisonment and being 'endorsed out' – which meant banished from the white areas and therefore from the source of employment.

Freedom of movement for the Jews and for blacks

Jews may not leave their places of dwelling after 9:00 p.m. in summer and after 8:00 p.m. in winter.

It is prohibited for Jews to leave their residential areas without having on their person written permission from their local police.

The Jews were then prohibited from entering certain areas reserved for 'Germans only', and, finally, they were placed in ghettos, each of which had its own detailed restrictions as to when and where the

Jews could move, some forbidding them to be on the streets at all between seven in the evening and seven o'clock the next morning.

Some of the most humiliating and certainly the most hated of all laws passed against the blacks by the Pretoria régime were the 'pass laws', a series of laws designed to have complete control over the movements of the black population and to keep them firmly within their own designated areas. This policy was known by the government as 'influx control'.

Besides enforcing curfews, the law also stipulated that no blacks could remain in a white area for more than 72 hours unless they fulfilled certain rigid residential qualifications.

Blacks had to carry their pass books on them at all times – even if they just crossed the road to visit a neighbour – and the book contained all his or her personal details, from the place of birth to fingerprints.

Police made pass raids at all times of the day and night, and anyone who was found without a pass was arrested. The numbers taken into police custody and detained for not having their passes on them were ridiculous. At one time the police were arresting on average nearly 2,000 people every day.

One African wrote, 'There are few aspects of European administration that Africans resent so bitterly as the pass laws and regulations. They consider passes as badges of inferiority; they resent the constant interference of the police; the fines imposed are out of all proportion to the offence or to the income of the offender and the conviction stands as a "previous conviction"'.

Freedom of expression

Not only was freedom of movement curtailed for the Jews and for the blacks, but freedom of expression also. The Nazis, having denied the Jews their right to vote, then passed laws which forbade them from publishing newspapers, magazines or from forming political organisations. In Nazi Germany, anyone who criticised the Third Reich was labelled 'communist'. They were in fact denied the fundamental right of expressing themselves freely. They became the voiceless ones.

The Nats, having come to power, wasted little time in disenfranchising the blacks. They, too, followed this by banning all black political organisations and closing down black newspapers. Anyone who criticised the Pretoria régime was labelled 'Communist'. Political leaders were exiled or imprisoned. The blacks, too, became voiceless in the land of their birth.

Police power

Police were given full authority to arrest and detain Jews without a warrant. Jews were denied the right to appear and be charged before a court of law. Nor did they have any right to sue for redress. The secret police, known as the Gestapo, were used extensively to terrorise the Jewish population.

The Nats gave the South African police full authority to search black premises and to arrest blacks (not whites) without a warrant. The Minister of Justice could detain, without trial, opponents of apartheid for an indefinite period. The secret police network is one of the most efficient in the world and organised police informers infiltrate every level of society.

Between 1984 and 1986 it was estimated that over 11,000 young people were detained without trial.

Father Trevor Huddleston wrote, just eight years after the Nats had come to power:

Hell is not a bad description of South Africa, nor a very great exaggeration. As I understand it theologically, the real pain and agony . . . of hell is frustration. Its atmosphere is dread. Its horror is its eternity. When you are in hell, you see the good but can never reach it; you know that you are made for God, but between yourself and him 'there is a great gulf fixed'. It is not a bad description of the ultimate meaning of apartheid. And I am not at all sure that it is very far from the ideal which the present Government of South Africa has set itself to actualise.

8

SURPRISED BY LOVE

Everywhere Ellen Faul goes, she leaves her mark. It's a mark that speaks of beauty and a love of luxury, and in this beauty and luxury she enfolds whoever enters her domain. Even now, living in the black township, with the army troop-carriers bullying outside, the sound of a gunshot, the roar and hubbub of evening traffic, her everyday cutlery is silver and the blankets on the spare beds are made of the softest mohair.

A day in her company, interlaced as it nearly always is with an equal quota of laughter and tears, can be as new and refreshing as a week's holiday. It is not unusual to leave her with some of your old conceptions swept away, and new questions left to be answered. But always you leave her feeling that you have been with someone who is truly alive, and who has passed on to you some of the complexity and vitality of living.

Ellen is 'all woman', as the Americans would say. At 60 she is still beautiful, her most striking feature being her eyes. There's nothing you can say about them that wouldn't sound corny. The truth is that they are large, they are sometimes blue and sometimes green, and they do brim over with both laughter and tears. In them you read an enjoyment of life, a sense of fun and lack of self-pity. When she cries, you know that it comes from an experience of pain or exhaustion that is for that moment too much to contain.

She is always immaculately dressed and made up and wears shoes with heels you feel must be too high for all the running around she does. And she does run. Or rather, trot. Getting ready to go anywhere is clearly for her one of the major crises of life, but one she's learnt to cope with good-naturedly. She will always be late and has adopted a little trotting run, accompanied by a slight puffing, which she uses to express the fact that she is actually hurrying and doing her best. It is not unusual to see Nico hanging around at the foot of the stairs, or hovering over an open newspaper with that look of controlled acceptance good husbands learn to adopt in the face of the unchangeable.

Part of the problem will arise from what to take – either for the day or the weekend. During a one-night stop-over in Venda, the mission hospital she and Nico built from scratch, she took with her – in her Mercedes-Benz – one medium-sized suitcase, packed full, and one vanity case as well as her large ostrich-skin handbag which looks like a rat's nest inside. When you point out that it's a rat's nest she says well maybe she needs a bigger bag. When you suggest that with a bigger bag she'd just have a bigger mess, she has to admit that this is most probably true.

Her ostrich-skin handbag she regards as an extension of herself, like a limb, and it's very reassuring for us lesser mortals, seeing this beautiful and well-turned-out lady, to know that if you opened half the drawers in her house, or her bag, you would find merry chaos inside.

Despite the galloping pace of her life as a consultant psychiatrist, she maintains an almost childlike delight in the pleasures of life. On our first meeting she rushed into the kitchen with a little packet held high above her head, eyes bright as a ferret's;

'I have found the entrails!' she cried jubilantly.

'Pardon?'

'The entrails. I have found the entrails.'

She and Nico were going on a camping holiday in a small van so packed full of gear (including a plastic bag with a pipe that you filled with water, left in the sun, then hooked on to a tree and stood under if you wanted a warm shower) that when you opened the back door half the stuff fell out. For some reason she wanted to make sausages from any game that was shot. It transpired that the entrails were the sausage skins, surprisingly available at our local butchery.

While supper is being made and the menfolk talking in the other room, Ellen engages in a long and animated conversation about inherited characteristics and with one swift movement raises her skirts to her waist to show you her beautiful legs, passed on, she says, through her mother. She displays them not with any pride, just with a sense of fun and a total lack of inhibition.

And then, quite suddenly, she'll switch off, leaving you as abruptly as she came, overcome with fatigue.

No wonder the young Nico, just graduated, emotionally shy, should find himself bowled over by a lady not only as deeply committed to Christ as he was, but beautiful and spontaneous as well. For him, it was love at first sight.

They met at a little country church where Nico was preaching. Ellen, a newly-qualified doctor, had reluctantly accompanied her parents. She was at a painful crossroads in her life. An only child, she was finally about to cut the umbilical cord that bound her to her self-willed and possessive mother.

Mrs Faul wanted her to take a country practice to be near at hand, but Ellen knew that if she was ever to stand on her own feet she had to get away. Not an easy situation to handle with a mother who used depression as a weapon to get her own way.

Not only that, but Ellen was struggling to come to terms with the turmoil caused by a loving but painful relationship that had not worked out. She was angry with God and deeply ill at ease.

That morning the young visiting preacher spoke about the peace God promises to those who love and obey him. As Nico preached Ellen felt the words were meant for her. She later had no recollection of the preacher, but only of the presence of God as he brought his promised peace and comfort to her heart.

After the service Nico and Ellen were introduced by a mutual friend. Absorbed in her feelings, it meant nothing to Ellen. But Nico, with uncharacteristic speed, soon found a pretence of visiting her parents' home, and within a week they were having supper together in a little restaurant, and Ellen found herself pouring out to this gentle young man all the pain and confusion she was suffering.

A profoundly religious woman with a high moral code which she applied as rigidly to herself as to other people, she couldn't get over how understanding and non-judgmental Nico was. For her a conversation that began with a minister, ended with a lover.

Nico, overwhelmed by her openness and naturalness, allowed his arm to be held as they walked home. Eleven months later they were married and there began a relationship of personal commitment and courage that was to take them through periods of worldly success and social acclaim, to the place of rejection and pain.

*   *   *

Ellen never wanted to be a clergy wife. The idea of having a parish house, which half the world and its dog felt entitled to make their second home, was not her idea of domestic bliss. A generous and loving person to her friends, she had nevertheless always found the idea of 'open house' quite threatening. She likes to know in the morning how many are likely to sit round her table that night. Nico, on the other hand (who, his children maintain, still cannot boil an egg), welcomes all comers to his hearth and to his table in the innocent expectation that food will materialise from somewhere to feed them all.

In the early days of their marriage Ellen would feel guilty and spiritually inferior because she felt she could not come up to Nico's expectations of, it seemed to her, unlimited energy and unlimited hospitality. The situation was made worse by the expectations of the congregation. Then, as now, congregations of most denominations tended to see their ministers' wives as an extension of their minister, an unpaid helper whose sole purpose in life was to meet the needs of the parish in whatever way they appeared. For a Dutch Reformed minister to marry a professional woman, especially a doctor, was somehow not quite done.

So for the first few years of their married life Ellen struggled with the expectations of the church, the demands of her generous but impractical husband, a part-time medical practice, and the needs of her growing family.

And then there was mother. Mrs Faul decided fairly early on that Nico was not good enough for her daughter. She expressed this by ignoring him as much as possible, even when a guest in their house, which she frequently was. She was also convinced that Ellen was incapable of running a home efficiently, and persistently interfered and undermined her daughter's self-confidence. Ellen's father was a gentle, educated man, but when he died she became the sole recipient of her mother's attention, and it was overwhelming.

Despite these difficulties, Ellen came from a loving and demonstrative family. Her two aunts were unmarried, so in a way Ellen was the only child of three sisters, the centre of their attention, used to giving and receiving love. Now she found herself married to a man whose spiritual stature she felt unable to meet, but who was almost incapable of showing her spontaneous physical affection.

'I think most of my brothers and sisters suffered from not being able to express their feelings,' says Nico. 'And you'd be surprised how many of us married only children, in search, I believe, of that real, deep, warm love.

'Ellen had a lot of love. In her home people hugged each other. She would just come and put her arms round me. It was so strange to me. I felt at home with them, but I just couldn't do it myself. In the beginning it was so difficult for Ellen to understand that. But I just couldn't. I used to feel guilty that God had given me to Ellen, when she needed someone who was so much more demonstrative than I.'

Nearly forty years of marriage have worked their miracles of change, but even now Ellen finds it hard when Nico becomes, as he calls it, 'formal', or withdraws from the company around him – often a sign that he's feeling depressed, or overworked. In the early days of their marriage she tried to force him out of it. Now she handles it more tactfully and Nico himself recognises when it's happening, and tries to respond.

Because she had always been the centre of attention, the

demands of Nico's life and personality have made Ellen more independent. His support and encouragement of her own professional life have enabled her to achieve. When her children were older she studied psychiatry and is now an assistant professor at the black hospital of Medunsa. None of that would have been possible without Nico behind her.

But though she, too, is ambitious and highly motivated, there is a difference in their orientation. Nico is totally immersed in the cause for which he has jeopardised their personal security and future. For Ellen, the central concern of her life was, is and always will be her relationship with Nico. If that is wrong, her whole world is out of kilter. If it is right, then everything is right and anything is possible.

Living with them, you cannot but be moved and inspired by their vision, slightly different though that may be for each, or by the strength of their bonding. Witness though it is to the power of Christian love, such absorption, in feelings and in causes, in some intimate way puts all the rest of us at arm's length – as their children were later to experience.

9

THE CHALLENGE OF VENDA

Even when Nico suffers periods of the darkest despair, the fundamental peace of God never leaves him. It has been the bedrock of his stormy life from that first moment as a boy when he knelt and gave his life to his Lord.

So strong was this experience of peace that it became the essence of his preaching during his first young years as a minister. Normally a man could not be ordained until he was 25, but Nico had been a precocious student and as a special concession they ordained him after graduation when he was still only 23. Almost immediately he received a call from a church in Johannesburg.

It was a huge church, over one thousand members, and it had problems. The outgoing dominie made it his proud boast that he had preached all the United Party supporters (the liberals) out of his congregation. That had suited the remaining members very well. The Afrikaners were so delighted by their new government that anyone who preached Afrikaner nationalism from the pulpit was more than welcome.

But that wasn't Nico's way. The church had become, especially in Afrikaner society, a social club that you attended to show the world you were a solid citizen. But Nico believed the church should be filled with the people of God, a converted people who knew what it meant to belong to the body of Christ, and who lived in the assurance of God's love for them, and with his underlying peace in their lives. He wanted to bring his congregation into a more intimate, vital relationship with the living God.

But he preached from a purely spiritual perspective. At that time he had no conception at all that social concern and involvement were essential ingredients of the Gospel. He had never been taught, and simply did not understand, that love for God without love for one's neighbour, was meaningless.

But he must have made his mark, for two and a half years later he received another call from a church in Potchefstroom in the Transvaal where Beyers Naudé was the pastor.

It was a rare opportunity. Potchefstroom was a university town and Nico had always wanted to work with students. This sort of position did not come your way very often. The church itself was the oldest in the province of the Transvaal and there was a lot of prestige attached to working for it. But the real pull was Beyers Naudé.

At that time there was no indication, at least to the outside world, that Beyers Naudé was turning rebel. He was Moderator of the Dutch Reformed Church in the Transvaal, which made him one of the most senior pastors in the land. He was a leading member of the Broederbond which his own father had helped to found. He was one of South Africa's favourite sons and appeared in every way to be a solid member of the Afrikaner establishment. He had been Nico's chaplain at university, and to be called to be co-pastor to a man so highly regarded was an honour indeed.

As it turned out it was to be more than an honour. It was to be an inspiration. Their time together was short, but Beyers was to lead the way through a wilderness Nico and Ellen were later to follow.

In 1963, after twenty-two years as a member, Naudé was publicly to renounce the Broederbond. In a letter to its chairman, Piet Meyer, which he made public, Naudé deplored Broederbond influence in the Church and its support of apartheid and the legislation enforcing it, which he said violated the Bible's demands for neighbourly love, justice and mercy.

He was thrown out of the Dutch Reformed Church, hounded by the Broederbond, harassed by the establishment, insulted in private and in public and finally put under house arrest for seven years. In the year that he and

Nico worked together, this unrest in Naudé was just beginning to tremble.

Nico recalls a day when Beyers had returned from one of his many trips to Johannesburg as Moderator. He had met, as he often did, with black church and political leaders, but this evening he was troubled. He told Nico that these men had been confronting him with realities that he just couldn't justify, with questions he couldn't answer.

'You know, Nico,' he said, 'whatever we may believe or say, 10 million people believing the opposite can't all be wrong. They live under the apartheid laws, and they experience them as oppressive. They can't all be wrong.'

'And that day,' says Nico, 'I knew that Beyers Naudé had crossed the bridge. He had lost his confidence in the system.'

They discussed the issue together many times, but they were both so entrenched in the concepts of their heritage, that they could not see any alternative to apartheid, even though they had begun to glimpse its inhumanity.

For Nico, enlightenment was still a long way off. All he could think at the time, was that the sooner the blacks left white South Africa and were resettled in their homelands, the happier they themselves would be. The thought of an integrated society remained an anathema.

Nico had not been at Potchefstroom a year before he was asked to attend a congress at Bloemfontein on the Tomlinson Report. The Tomlinson Report was a commission of inquiry set up by the government in 1956 to try to work out exactly where the homelands should be, how they should be structured, financed, and so on.

During the course of the congress Nico heard for the first time that only ten per cent of blacks living in the homelands were Christians. It really shook him. What right had he to live contentedly among the whites who already knew the Gospel, when ninety per cent of the blacks outside had never heard of Jesus Christ?

When he got home he told Ellen and for some days they began to pray that the Lord would raise up missionaries willing to go to the homelands with the message of Christ.

A week or so later they packed their bags for a holiday in the Kruger National Park, little suspecting what was to come.

Holidays always presented problems to the Smiths. For one thing Ellen had to decide what to pack. Then she had to try to leave at the prescribed time. Nico, on the other hand, floundered rather hopelessly in the domestic tasks presented to him and, once off, would drive relentlessly for hours on end impervious to the cries of wife and children who were hungry and tired in the back. The ensuing family fracas he would take in his stride, saying that since he and Ellen were such good friends – he would use the word comrades – they could weather the arguments without any difficulty.

Over the years the stress of getting off on holiday was such that Ellen drafted a letter designed, she said, to 'save the marriage' – a letter she unearthed again only the other day and read with great delight to her children.

Statement of N.J. and E. Smith

Bearing in mind the idiom that a donkey doesn't hurt itself twice on the same stone, and that the idiom is meant for donkeys, N.J. and E. Smith will undertake the following:

1. Never again to make a time to leave in the morning. 'Early' will only mean between 12 midnight and 7am, and the 7am limit will only be a vague approximation of the final parameters of 'early'.

2. Never ever will they depart from their home without saying very clearly in words that both will understand, which will be the place of the next meal.

3. As N.J. can live for 24 hours without food, and E. can only survive 4 hours without food, it is now undertaken to eat 3 times in 24 hours. This is a special concession from N.J. and E. acknowledges this with thanks.

4. We won't use the word 'comrade' any longer. We'll use the word 'spouse'.

Signed: N.J. and E. Smith

Their time at the National Park was, as usual, delightful, and on the way home they called on their old friend Carel

Boshoff and his wife, Anna, who was the daughter of Hendrik Verwoerd.

During the long car journeys their minds had turned again to the problem of evangelising the homelands, and it occurred to Nico that they had been praying very conveniently.

'Ellen,' he said, 'do we really have any right to ask God to make people willing to go to the blacks if we are not willing to go ourselves?'

'Well', said Ellen, 'let's just add that if the Lord wants us to go, he makes us willing and opens a door to us.' So they did. And never thought any more about it.

The Boshoffs were, as always, delighted to see them. Anna was her rather formal self, but Carel, as big as a bear and as warm in his embrace, beamed on them as they entered the house.

'How funny you should call now,' Anna said, 'we were just talking about you this morning. My father has told us of a place in the Northern Transvaal on the borders of Rhodesia where there is a desperate need for mission work and a hospital. They've no facilities at all. We thought how lovely it would be if you two could go.'

Slightly stunned they immediately said, No. Impossible. They had only been at their new parish one year. It was too early to move. Who would commission them? Where would the money come from? There was no shortage of valid reasons to say, categorically, No.

Two weeks later, unable to find any peace, Nico rang Carel and said they were ready to have a look.

The three of them went up together. Venda is right on the northern border of South Africa in a very secluded area. There were at that time about half a million people living there, very tribal in their life style and culture. Most of the land was owned by local tribes and the chiefs were not at all impressed by these three whites trying to find a patch of ground to build a hospital. It had to be the right patch, too, near suitable water and not too distant from the settlements.

Dispirited they returned home, deciding to ring Verwoerd – who at that time was Minister of Native

Affairs – on the way and ask to see him. Maybe he would have some ideas. Verwoerd said of course they could call, but he wouldn't be free until after 11pm that night.

For such a forceful man Verwoerd had a very mild manner. He'd be willing to discuss with you in detail matters in which you differed; sharing ideas was a delight to him but, if you attended a meeting at which he was present and you didn't know your facts, he'd dismiss you out of hand and tell you not to come back until you'd done your homework. Nico got on with him well, but always made sure that he was on his toes whenever they met.

This evening he greeted them all in his study, curious to know what was so urgent that they were prepared to visit him so late in the evening and then drive through the night to get home.

He heard them out. 'Give me three days, and I'll come back to you,' he said. And three days later, true to his word, Verwoerd phoned. They had found twelve morgens of land – about fifteen acres – that belonged to the government. It was the only possible place available, but it was thick bush, more like jungle. He doubted if they could use it, but they were welcome to try.

That same day Nico visited the Mission Secretary of the Church and explained that they were considering going to the mission field, but had no money. What was the possibility of the Church's financing them? 'None,' said the Mission Secretary, 'we have no money at all.' But before Nico left he bowed his head and said, so simply, 'Lord, if you want these people to go, please provide for their needs.'

So that was it. Nico and Ellen found themselves hoist, as it were, with their own petard. They'd worked themselves up about the need for the blacks to be evangelised. They had prayed for God to call missionaries. They had reluctantly and unconvincingly suggested themselves, and now here they were, a doctor and a priest, presented with a homeland needing a mission station and a hospital, twelve morgens of land and government permission.

What they didn't have was any official church backing or any money. They had no home to go to, no facilities laid on and no labour provided. If they decided to go then they would have to live by faith, with their small baby, camp out in a broken-down rondavel and physically clear fifteen acres of jungle with their bare hands. They would be the only whites living among half a million blacks whose language they did not speak and whose culture they did not understand. And they had three days to tell Verwoerd yes or no.

What really stressed Ellen was the lack of money. 'Nico,' she cried, 'for myself I can put up with anything. But how can I tell my baby that I have no bread for her mouth?'

That Saturday morning as they were on their knees praying about it, there was a ring at the front door. Nico went to answer it. There on the doorstep was one of their closest friends from the Church.

'I've baked you some buns,' she said, 'and for some reason this morning when I was praying for you, I felt the Lord tell me to bring you this,' and, looking a little perplexed, the friend handed Nico a ten-shilling note.

So this then was the answer to their cry. The Lord would provide.

Beyers Naudé gave them his heartfelt approval; the congregation were stunned, not just at losing him, but at the thought of him wasting his talents on the blacks, and Ellen's mother went into an instant depression.

That was May 1956. Their plans were announced in the papers and money began to trickle in. The Church pledged them $150 a month for the first year which would at least give them food to eat.

And so, on a wet August night they set off in their second-hand pickup for the long drive to Venda. Following close behind was a huge truck filled with all their worldly possessions. Where they were going to put them at the other end was another matter.

10

THE PLACE OF MERCY

In a thatched rondavel near the banana plantation, a young black Jew lay dreaming. Johannes Netshikulwe was used to dreams. He'd had them many times before, and in any case they were a part of the heritage of his people that he tried to read about in the family Bible.

The Netshikulwes were members of the Lemba Priesthood tribe and believed themselves to be part of the lost tribes of Israel. They lived and worshipped as Jews, and cherished their traditions in lonely isolation.

This night Johannes dreamt that white men from the Department of Native Affairs came and said that he must go and clear a patch of ground for a new hospital. In his dream Johannes went to a place a few kilometres down the road and began to clear the ground, but was told that he must not cut down the big trees, just the bush between them.

A week or two later the dream came true. Real men came to see him in his working hours – they were the men from the ministry sent by Verwoerd. They asked Johannes if he knew of the land owned by the government. They wanted to see if there was a suitable plot on it for a new hospital. So Johannes took them down the road to the place he had seen in his dream. And the men liked the place and said it might do, if they could only clear the bush.

And so Johannes knew that the hand of God was in this hospital, and he waited. He waited three months until one morning, at about eleven o'clock, a small van drew to a halt outside the remains of an old brick rondavel by the side of the dirt-road.

News of its arrival spread quickly through the settlement and he hurried along, and watched from the trees as a young white couple and their baby picked their way through the muddy field to the house.

The house was shaped like a dog's bone – two rondavels, or round rooms, joined by a narrow middle section that can't have been more than eight feet by twelve. The roof was thatched and reasonably watertight, but there were no windows or doors left intact.

The place had been used by the ministry during a campaign to eradicate malaria, and there was an old black wood-burning stove that still functioned, a water pump that didn't, and an outside latrine.

The rain had stopped by the time Nico, Ellen, and baby Maretha arrived, but the ground was sodden and the concrete floors of the rondavel were puddled with water where the rain had beaten through the window and door-frames. The house itself had been built on a flat patch of land, cleared of trees. Around them curved the arm of the hills, heavily wooded and glistening now from the heavy rains.

The jungle at Venda isn't heavy and sweaty. It's a dense but gentle tangle of hanging vines and undergrowth, of thick evergreen plants sprawling up the trunks of deciduous trees. The hedgerows are more like an English country lane, with brambles and wild clematis and what looks like rose bay willow herb, tumbling and scruffing together, all fighting for breathing space among the wayside shrubs.

There are long stretches of banana plantations, their shaggy leaves low cropped, and lemon and mango groves and clumps of the huge lychee tree. The neat rows of the orange groves make the fields look, from a distance, as if they've been combed.

As Nico and Ellen waited for their furniture to arrive the sun came out, shafting through the tall trees, picking up particles of dust from the Devon-red soil and the smoke from the kraal fires. More and more villagers began to gather among the trees, watching them, too nervous to come near them, amazed that these white strangers should suddenly have arrived.

But when their furniture van eventually drew up and they began to unload, piling the chairs and the tables, the lamps and the china and everything else on to the wet grass, from out of the crowd slipped Johannes Netshikulwe. He spoke a little English, and with the willingness of one knowing he was doing God's will, he began to help the Smiths dry the floors and move the furniture.

He was to become Nico's right-hand man, helping him with the manual work and giving him valuable advice about the people of Venda. He was soon to accept Christianity, and he is still at the hospital today, in charge of the laundry complex, thirty years after he first began work in his dream.

When they realised that they had no water, quite apart from windows and doors, Nico and Ellen decided that there was nothing for it but to drive back and wait for the ministry to carry out the repairs. Turning their little van around, they drove back along the dirt-road, through the long night to Pretoria.

A week later they were finally installed, the water flowing, the house whitewashed and repaired. As they lay in bed that first night, listening to the unfamiliar sounds of the jungle, Nico could not sleep.

'I thought dear Lord, what are we doing here? But the Lord just carried us through.'

A real pilgrimage, says Nico, is one where you walk out in faith and believe that God will undertake for you, that he will not leave you in the lurch. Having taken that step of faith once, it's never so hard to do again. It brings you a new freedom. You realise that you really can trust God. The way may not always be easy, but the Lord is faithful and he will give you strength.

Almost immediately Nico applied to the Department of Health for permission to build a TB hospital. The Department agreed to support them by contributing £7 for every £1 raised from other sources. Nico spread the word and soon the money was flowing in. He and Johannes began to clear the ground in preparation for the foundations. The smaller trees had to be rooted out and the land cleared of boulders. It was an awesome task. A small workforce from the African settlement began to help them and eventually Nico was able to buy the necessary equipment.

Those first six months were particularly exciting for Ellen. News that there was a doctor around spread rapidly through the community. On their first morning they woke to find an old man sitting on their doorstep. He said he'd come because he'd heard there was a doctor in the house and could she come and help his cow. The cow had swallowed a mango that had got stuck in its gullet.

Piling into the truck, Ellen and Nico drove the six miles to the old man's plot and found the cow. Ellen had brought with her a bottle of olive oil which she poured down the cow's throat as Nico and the farmer pinned it to the ground. Later that afternoon they went back, worked the mango up the cow's now well-lubricated gullet, and pulled it out.

Day by day the queue outside their house grew. The people came to Ellen for every conceivable ailment from infections to infertility.

There was a dilapidated storeroom near by, and this Ellen cleaned up and used as her first clinic, examining patients on the floor and treating them with the store of drugs that she had brought with her. If ever an operation was called for, Ellen would take them in the truck to the nearest hospital.

Because of the obvious need it was decided that Nico's first building should be a clinic for Ellen. Soon a nurse joined her and the practice grew.

Both of them worked flat out, Ellen on her growing medical practice and planning the medical facilities needed for the new hospital, Nico with the actual building, the fund raising, and coping with the mass of paperwork that resulted from it all. They soon had a huge number of individuals and organisations sponsoring the work, and Nico insisted on writing them all personal thank-you letters. He worked by paraffin lamp way into the night.

After six months Ellen fell pregnant with their second child. Pregnancy always made her very nauseous. At first she tried to carry on, but she grew steadily more depressed and Nico was too preoccupied to give her the sort of attention she felt she deserved. One day, in a fit of misery, she took herself off into the bush and sat under a tree feeling sorry for herself.

'I sat there for two hours and bemoaned my lot,' she'll tell you now, enjoying the memory, 'but nobody came to look for me, so I just had to go back and get on with it!'

But it was clear that she could not continue at such a pace through her pregnancy. She took herself and Maretha off to Potchefstroom for a few weeks to stay with a friend until the worst of the sickness had passed, leaving Nico to burn the midnight paraffin on his own.

Not much more than a year after their arrival, Nico and Ellen gave birth to their second daughter, Eduan, and their first hospital ward of 120 beds for TB patients.

By the time the Smiths left, seven years later, their family had sprouted another daughter, Linkie, and the TB ward had blossomed into a general hospital with a total of five hundred beds, a psychiatric unit and a ward for the chronically sick. It had a medical staff of nearly forty doctors and nurses and employed going on for 150 local people.

The grounds had also acquired a considerable reputation. Nico had been adamant that the big trees should not be cut down, and he planned the wards, outhouses and staff accommodation to fit in with the jungle. The result was a wild parkland of indigenous trees and natural undergrowth with lawns and shrubberies carefully designed by Ellen to give colour and grace to the natural environment.

Looking back on it now, Ellen and Nico never speak of those years without saying that they were only possible through the grace of God. Other hospitals have subsequently sprung up in the region, all named after their founders. The Smiths' hospital was named 'Dshilidzini', which means, in the Venda language, 'The Place of Mercy'. When the wing for the chronically sick was built the local people themselves had a name all ready, 'Khathutshelo', meaning 'The Place of Compassion'.

Nico and Ellen never talk of 'their' hospital, only of a time in their lives when the Lord upheld them, and gave them his peace and his strength to carry on.

11

THE STORK AND THE FOX

The starting up of the church, however, was a different story, and there was many a time when Nico came close to despair.

For the first three years at Venda, almost nothing happened spiritually. To begin with Nico held his services out of doors, often moving from place to place. He and Johannes visited every hut and invited the people to come. And at first they did, in good number. Nico decided he'd begin at the beginning, and so he started to tell them about God and how he created the world. Sunday by Sunday he reeled out the creation story.

But something was wrong. Each week the numbers who attended grew fewer and fewer until eventually there was no one left at all. The people of Venda were clearly not interested in either Nico or his God.

It was a dreadful blow to a young man who had always succeeded in everything he tried, and who prided himself on his power to preach. He sat down with Johannes and asked his advice.

'You are telling them what they already know,' said Johannes. 'They already believe in a God who created the earth. And they still believe that he is ruling this world. You're not telling them anything they haven't heard from childhood. Why should they come to hear you tell them what they already know?'

What Nico discovered was that he had a completely wrong concept of non-Christian people who had their own religion. He had this naïve idea that blacks were just waiting to reach out to the Christian faith, all you had to do was offer them the Bible, and they'd grab at it!

As he and Johannes talked he realised that the people of Venda knew that God created the universe and was in ultimate control, but that he was a distant and shadowy figure to them; a God to whom they could not relate, and to whom they did not feel drawn. A God who didn't seem to have anything to do with their daily lives.

Far more real to them were their ancestors, whose spirits they worshipped, and whom they believed interceded with God the creator on their behalf. It was the ancestral spirits you had to obey and mollify and appease, and if you angered the spirits, which was not difficult, then you could expect sickness and trouble and drought. They were far more interested in how to get on with the spirits, than they were about this impersonal and amorphous God.

This realisation threw Nico. He had to rethink his whole approach to proclaiming the Gospel and it took him a long time before he realised that he must begin not with God but with Jesus Christ. Like St Paul, he decided to preach one thing only, 'Christ crucified'. And so, Sunday by Sunday, first in one settlement, then in another, Nico unfolded the story of Jesus Christ. He told them who he was and where he came from. He told them that he healed the sick and cast out evil spirits; that he died and rose from the dead. And he told them the things that Jesus said about our life on earth and our relationship to him.

Nico had little or no respect for the Venda culture. In his heart of hearts he thought it fairly worthless and felt they would reject it completely when they'd been taught something better, but he was wise enough not to denigrate their spiritual beliefs. Rather he tried to bring them into line with the Gospel message.

One day he was preaching among a group of huts where he often went, and an old alcoholic was sitting on a boulder away from the rest. Nico had taken a legend from their own history to explain what Christ's death on the cross really meant.

One of the kings of the Swazi had come from the south to wage war against the people of Venda and eventually he conquered them. But in the fighting the king had been wounded in the hand. After the battle he stood up and raised his hand so that the people could see his blood dripping on the land.

'You see my blood,' he said, 'falling on the earth? Now this earth is part of me because my blood has fallen on it. This country, and all of you who live in it, now belong to me, because I have shed my blood to win you.'

Nico explained that when Christ died on the cross his blood was shed for all of us, that we might belong to him. He was king of this world and had won us by his wounds. When he had finished the old man rose from his boulder and came to Nico.

'If what you say is true,' he said, 'and Jesus is the king of this world, and I belong to him, then I must come to him.'

That old alcoholic was the first person in Venda to be baptised. He never did sit with the rest of the village, preferring always to perch on his boulder at the edge of the crowd, but he never looked back, and Nico is sure that over the years he really came to understand about Christ in his heart and the power of the Holy Spirit in his life.

Nico built a little church and furnished it with wooden benches and a black evangelist came to join those who spoke the Venda language.

Not long after the old man had been baptised there was a terrible drought, and the Ministry asked them if they would take a number of the older women into service on the mission station, just to clean up leaves, or do light tasks, so that they could be paid a wage in order to survive. Nico announced that anyone wanting work should be at the early morning service at 7am each day.

'I can still remember that first morning,' he says. 'About sixty women turned up, most of whom had never been to a church in their lives. Some were sitting on the benches with their backs to the pulpit. Others had their feet tucked up under them, looking most uncomfortable, because they didn't know that you kept your feet on the ground!'

Nico made it a rule that if they wanted work, they met in the church first, and during these times he continued his stories about Jesus Christ.

One morning, at about three o'clock, the young

evangelist got up to use the outside toilet. As he opened his front door he found an old woman with a bent back, sitting on the ground waiting.

'What is the matter, Mother?' he asked. 'Are you all right?'

'It's that man Jesus,' she said. 'I have just heard about him for the first time, and in the night I heard a voice telling me that I must believe in him, and I couldn't sleep. In the end I said, yes, I wanted to believe in him, but what must I do to believe? So I decided to come here and wait for you to wake, then you would tell me.'

That little old lady was one of the first. She came through to a living faith in Christ. She would witness to the catechism class, walking into the church with her back bent double. Her presence gave Nico enormous encouragement, and helped to bring many others to an understanding of the love of God. Slowly the church gathered momentum.

But during those first three years of spiritual barrenness Nico had many moments of despair. He had tried everything he knew, to no avail. At times his life seemed to be all administration. What was the point, he asked the Lord, of seven years' theological training if all he was going to do in the end was make bricks and push paper? Yet, paradoxically, there was also great satisfaction in seeing bricks turn into buildings, and buildings into hospital wards, and to be part of a whole factory of activity.

As the church began to grow, and more people came to accept the Christian message, Nico realised he had learnt an important lesson; that you can't force people to believe. Neither was it a matter of his personal skill as a preacher or teacher. He of himself was powerless. The work of conversion belonged to God the Holy Spirit alone. It was with renewed humbleness that he watched the benches fill up on Sunday mornings and heard the Venda people praising God in their own tongue.

Looking back now, what grieves him most is the poverty of his relationships with the blacks with whom he lived and worked. He was totally paternalistic. He was the boss, and he ran the show. Johannes once tried to point out to him that if he wanted the people to believe in Christianity, then he had to look like what he was talking about. It was no good preaching about brotherly love if he didn't act brotherly love.

But Nico could see nothing wrong with his attitude. He was there, wasn't he, working for them, doing his best to introduce them to Christ and to ease their transition into the Western world? He was blind to the possibility that maybe the Venda people had something to teach him, or that although he lived among them, he did not live with them.

'We were really like the typical colonisers Jean-Paul Sartre talks about who colonise an area and then create their own world in the midst of it. We were operating our own system of apartheid.'

He refused to allow any mixing of the races on the mission station. Blacks and whites had to eat separately and were not allowed to meet at social functions. In effect he created two worlds on the station, with blacks living on one side and whites on the other.

'Our understanding of the Gospel then was not that you identified with a person, only that you associated with them in order to preach the Gospel.'

Their insensitivity to the people they lived and worked among is epitomised in a story Nico now tells against himself, with great shame.

The black nurses at the hospital, wanting to build more meaningful relationships with the white staff, invited the whites to a meal in the nurses' home. Sensitive to the feelings of the Afrikaners, they did not sit down themselves to eat, instead they prepared the food and served it to their guests as a gesture of friendship.

But before the dinner, one of the white doctors went to see Nico, very agitated, and said this was a dangerous precedent and Nico must say something at the dinner which made it clear to the nurses that while it was very kind of them to make such a gesture, it really should not be repeated.

So in his speech of 'thanks', Nico told the nurses the story of the fox and the stork. The fox invited the stork to a meal, but served it all on flat plates, so the stork, with his long beak, found it impossible to eat. The stork then invited the fox to a meal, and served the food in deep bowls, so that the fox, with his short snout, found that he could not eat.

'In this way I tried to tell them that we were foxes and storks, and we just couldn't eat together.'

Perhaps the most telling anecdote of their lack of real love concerns the old man who worked in their house. One weekend the Smiths were travelling to Pretoria – a good eight hours' drive – and he asked if he could go with them to visit his daughter who was living there. They hardly ever met because he couldn't get to Pretoria, and he'd love to see her.

The Smiths didn't even consider it. They just said, No. There was no way they could travel with a black man in their car. And that was the end of it.

But their time of complacency was coming to an end. A small but significant incident took place before they left Venda, which was to trigger off the revolution in their lives.

An ecumenical meeting of church leaders was called, which Nico was asked to attend. At the meeting were black and white clergy from a variety of different churches in South Africa. When it came to lunch-time, Nico was horrified to see that the dining room had been laid in such a way that they were clearly all expected to eat together. And Nico couldn't. Psychologically he found himself unable to sit down with a black man and eat.

The German pastor's wife in whose home this took place noticed Nico's distress and said: 'Don't worry Mr Smith, I've laid a place for you in my husband's study.'

So Nico ate in isolation in his host's study, his first reaction being one of self-righteousness that at least he still knew what the Gospel of Christ stood for, and didn't these others realise that by eating together they were on the slippery slope of fraternisation that could lead to a sinful intimacy?

But after his initial glow of self-congratulation an uneasy feeling began to permeate his mind that maybe he was not quite as right as he thought he was. After all, they all preached the same Gospel, and there they were, free and together, and here was he, alone.

The day passed, but the memory of it lingered, and was to come back to haunt him in the months that lay ahead.

Seven years after their arrival in Venda Nico was asked if he would take on the role of mission secretary for the Northern Transvaal. That would mean taking responsibility for all the mission stations and missionaries operating in the area – a huge task.

But it seemed right. The church now had a healthy congregation of more than four hundred Christians. The hospital was well established with a steady flow of foreign doctors and students supplementing the local staff. He and Ellen had done what they came for. It was time to move on.

In accepting the post of mission secretary he made one proviso – that he could first spend three months in Europe. Neither of them had been out of Africa, and he wanted to see how the Europeans tackled their missionary work, and pick up new stimulus and new ideas.

He also wanted to meet Karl Barth.

12

A PROPHETIC INTERVIEW

Karl Barth was the spiritual inspiration behind the German Confessing Church that emerged during the Third Reich in resistance to the policies of National Socialism. A German Swiss, he was regarded as one of the most significant theologians of his time and did more than anyone else to reveal the shallowness of prevalent humanistic doctrines.

During the nineteenth century the liberal theologians had reduced Jesus to a mere man, albeit with a super spirituality. They built their theology around Christ the man, and not Christ as God. Jesus was an ethical teacher, just more open to God than other men.

They interpreted the Bible according to the intellectual patterns of their age, and so, being a scientific age, there were no miracles. Instead there were logical scientific explanations for what occurred. The virgin birth was part of ancient myth, the resurrection was allegorical, there was no scientific proof of the intervention of a transcendental God into the history of the world.

Darwin's theory of evolution implied that mankind was evolving all the time. He had now reached a stage of moral enlightenment and the problems of the world were caused by ignorance, not by any forces of evil. There was no cosmic battle between good and evil, there was no inherently destructive side of man's nature that could not be enlightened by education. Man had a God consciousness and Jesus was the epitome of a man with such an awareness.

They had reduced the Gospel to the level of positive humanism and did not feel that the future of man was endangered. Many leading theologians joined forces with the intellectuals of the day to support the Kaiser's policies and launched into the First World War in the confidence that mankind was now able to make moral and just decisions that would benefit society as a whole without recourse to illusionary supernatural intervention.

Barth was vehemently against this view. He saw the folly in mankind, their propensity to evil – a view that can only have been reinforced as he watched Germany move through the thirties and forties. He believed in a God who had revealed himself through Scripture, who had made himself known through Jesus Christ, and through whom there was a possibility of grace.

He believed in a God who was in control of the universe and under whose judgment all that was in the universe would fall. Christ was not a mere man, but God incarnate, and faith in God was not some primitive instinct, but a gift that God himself imparted through his Holy Spirit. God was alive and came to individual men and women and set them free.

Barth's opposition to Hitler and National Socialism was unremitting. When, in 1934, Hitler tried to make every pastor and church official take an oath of loyalty that they would, '. . . as befitting a servant of the Gospel in the German Protestant Church, be faithful and obedient to the leader of the German *Volk* and state, Adolf Hitler, and . . . pledge to serve him . . .' Barth refused.

Writing a personal letter to Hitler, Barth explained that his highest loyalty was not to an earthly Führer, but to Jesus Christ, the son of God. He could only obey Hitler if what he was asked to do and say were not contrary to the Gospel of Christ.

Because of Barth's intellectual standing in Europe, Hitler realised that he had here a formidable opponent. He gave him twenty-four hours to be outside the borders of Germany.

Nico had been deeply attracted to Barth's theology. 'I always thought, in my small little religious world, that faith was all about God and me. God was available to me, and I could ask him to do all sorts of things on my behalf.

Barth made me realise that God was God himself, with or without my help, and that he was in charge, determining what was going to happen. I was in his service, not he in mine.'

When he and Ellen arrived in Basle he went to the mission office and mentioned that he would love to meet Professor Barth.

'Oh,' said the secretary, 'you'd like to meet Karl? Hang on.' And so saying he picked up the phone and dialled a number.

'Karl, there's a young missionary here from South Africa who'd like to meet you. Can he come over?'

It was as simple as that. The secretary told Nico what bus to take and within an hour he was ringing the bell of a modest, two-storey house.

'When he opened the door I couldn't believe it. He looked like an old farmer! He had a tough, weather-beaten face and crumpled clothes. Anyone would think he'd just come off the land. Outwardly, there was nothing impressive about him at all. And he was deeply humble. "So," I thought, "this is Karl Barth, the greatest theologian in the world!"'

Barth lead Nico into his study. There were books everywhere: on the floor, on the chairs, on his desk, lining the walls. Clearly this was a factory for thinking. Barth, sucking gently at his pipe, set the ball rolling.

'It's interesting that you should come now, from South Africa,' he said, 'because about a week ago I was reading a speech made by your Prime Minister Verwoerd on race relations and I was amazed because he was saying almost the very same things that President Davies of the Southern States of America said about their race relations exactly 100 years ago. Am I to believe that South Africa is 100 years behind the times?'

This was too much for Nico. He was still very sensitive and didn't want anyone to criticise either his country, or apartheid – especially the man he'd travelled half the world to meet. So he laughed rather nervously and passed the comment off and moved on to the subject of theology.

And that's where they stayed, for an hour or more,

Barth immensely humble and self-effacing, and avoiding any topic that he felt might embarrass his young disciple. But as Nico rose to leave the old man put the question that was to change Nico's life.

'May I ask you a personal question?' he said. 'Are you free to preach the Gospel in South Africa?'

'But of course,' said Nico, rather taken aback. 'We have freedom of religion in my country. There's no problem about that.'

'Yes,' said Barth, 'but it's not as easy as that. Supposing the Holy Spirit were to reveal to you an understanding of the Gospel that your friends and family did not like; an understanding that they did not want you to proclaim. Are you free enough to be faithful to what the Holy Spirit reveals to you?'

Nico was perplexed. What was he driving at? 'I really don't know,' he said. 'I'm not in that position. I'm accepted as I am and people believe in what I preach.'

'Yes,' said Barth again, 'but it may become even more difficult than that. You may at some stage discover teachings in the Gospel which are contrary to what your government believes. Are you so free that even then you will say that you must be faithful to the Gospel and preach it as the Holy Spirit reveals?'

By this time Nico was very embarrassed indeed. 'I don't know,' he said, 'I don't know what my reaction would be.'

And Barth said, 'That's all right then,' and putting his hand on Nico's shoulder, saw him to the door, and smiled his goodbye.

Three times Barth had asked him, 'Are you free?' As he turned the conversation over in his mind Nico found himself thinking of the conversation Jesus had had with Simon Peter on the beach, after his resurrection:

'Simon, son of John, do you love me more than these others do?'

'Yes, Lord, you know that I love you.'

Jesus said to him, 'Take care of my lambs.' And a second time Jesus said to him, 'Simon, son of John, do you love me?'

'Yes, Lord,' he answered, 'you know that I love you.'

Jesus said to him, 'Take care of my sheep.' A third time Jesus said, 'Simon, son of John, do you love me?'

Peter was sad because Jesus asked him the third time, 'Do you love me?' so he said to him, 'Lord, you know everything; you know that I love you!'

Jesus said to him, 'Take care of my sheep. I am telling you the truth: when you were young, you used to get ready and go anywhere you wanted to; but when you are old, you will stretch out your hands and someone else will bind you and take you where you don't want to go.' Then Jesus said to him, 'Follow me.'

Nico left that interview with Barth, still justifying his own position, still finding excuses for apartheid. He said to himself that South Africa was not like Nazi Germany had been, and so what Barth had been through, what he had said, was not really applicable to him.

But deep in his heart there was now a question that he could not answer, 'Am I really free? Am I free to preach the Gospel? Am I really free from all other bondage?' It was a question that would not go away.

Karl Barth did not live long enough to know how prophetic his words to Nico had been. But his son, Marcus, himself a professor of theology, was one of the first to write Nico a letter of encouragement when he and Ellen finally moved outside the gate, to Mamelodi.

13

THE BROTHERHOOD AND
THE TYPHOON

The following year Nico was invited to join the Afrikaner Broederbond. He didn't know it, but for eighteen months or more his professional and personal life had been under intimate scrutiny.

Before the Brotherhood will even contemplate inviting a man to join them, they carry out a sophisticated surveillance of every aspect of his life. They discover his strengths, his weaknesses, his affiliations, his background, his habits, even the details of his family life – all unbeknown to him.

They make stringent demands in terms of cultural, family, moral, religious and political activities. For example, no one will be admitted, however staunch an Afrikaner national, if he has married an English-speaking woman. Nor are they acceptable if they've been to an English-speaking school, or belong to sports clubs with too many English-speaking members.

Regular church attendance is essential, but it must be at one of the Afrikaner establishment denominations. Any form of Sunday sport or recreation is likely to debar a man from admission and as for divorce, not only will a divorced man not be considered, but should a Broederbonder divorce when a member, he will be thrown out unless the circumstances are very exceptional. It goes without saying that the 'target recruit' must also be a member of the right political party.

Anyone nominating a recruit is asked to be 'convinced' that he:

strives for the perpetuation of a separate Afrikaner nation with its own language and culture; that he gives preference to Afrikaners and other well-disposed people and companies in the economic, public and professional fields; that he upholds the Afrikaans language at home, in his job and his community at large; that he is a Protestant; that there is nothing in his personality, character or behaviour that would make him unsuitable for membership; that he is exceptionally trustworthy, principled and prudent; that he can meet the financial implications of membership; that he is able and willing to take an active, regular and loyal part in all the organisation's activities; and that he does not belong to any other secret or semi-secret organisation.

If the unsuspecting target gets through all this, he is then approached by two or three Broeders who know him personally and put out discreet feelers to test his attitude towards the Broederbond, though no details of the organisation are given. If he seems amenable, the information committee takes over the recruitment, stopping it at any stage if they feel the target recruit is not responding in the right way.

The recruit, even when he accepts membership (and no one is approached unless his acceptance is considered a foregone conclusion), still knows very little about the organisation he has agreed to join. He can be told that admission is by invitation only; the contents of the constitution; the existence (but not the details) of a programme of action; the composition of members of the society who belong to the Broederbond, like ministers, doctors, professors, farmers, artisans, lawyers, advocates, teachers, etc, but not their names. He is then told that he must pay R40 on admission and R20 per year as well as any levies the executive council may impose.

When Nico was approached, quite innocent of all the prying that had been going on into his public and private life, he was, like most of the uninitiated, very ignorant about the Broederbond's true nature. He thought it was just a service organisation, like the

Round Table, but promoting Afrikaner interests and strengthening Afrikaner culture. He had no idea that it was socially manipulative or any notion of the corruptive political power that it could wield.

Even so, he was hesitant. He told the people who came to see him that he felt he didn't know enough about it. He was uneasy with a secret society.

Why should he be, they argued. The Moderator of the Church was a member. So was his old friend Beyers Naudé. Dr Treurnicht was a member. Many ministers in the Dutch Reformed Church were Broeders. How could it be un-Christian when so many Church leaders were a part of it?

So Nico joined, much against Ellen's wishes. She was still convinced that anything secret could not be godly.

In the late seventies Ivor Wilkins and Hans Strydom, two South African journalists, produced their remarkable book called *The Super-Afrikaners*, which revealed for the first time the workings and membership of the Afrikaner Broederbond. Their courage and tenacity were on a par with those journalists who first broke the American Watergate scandal at such risk to themselves and their informers, and it blew the Bond sky-high.

In it they describe the induction ceremony as 'a darkly dramatic affair', ending, as it does, with a sacred oath before God to carry the secrets of the organisation to the grave.

As the new recruit stands on the threshold of admission to the ranks of the Super-Afrikaners, his knowledge of them is scant and vague. They have framed the ceremony with a caution which is typical of all their activities. Like the recruitment process, it has several cut-off points so that the recruit is exposed gradually to revelations of the organisation's inner secrets. At each of these points he must acknowledge that he is in accord with everything he has heard so far and wishes the induction to proceed to the next phase.

The modern ceremony is less bizarre than the early version, during which there was a dramatic rite with a 'body'

on a bier transfixed with a dagger. The dummy's winding-
sheet had the word 'verraad' (treason) embroidered on it in
blood red. Every member had to stab it with a dagger,
symbolically indicating the penalty of betrayal.

The 'Chaplain' conducting the ceremony intoned: 'He
who betrays the Bond will be destroyed by the Bond. The
Bond never forgets. Its vengeance is swift and sure. Never
yet has a traitor escaped his just punishment.'

While the modern version of the initiation ceremony is a
little less macabre it remains, say Wilkins and Strydom,
'A chilling affair that could come straight from the pages
of fiction.' The cult of secrecy is still so deeply embedded in
its members, that even though their membership has
now been publicly revealed, many will react with startled
horror when you mention it to them outright.

The new ceremony takes place at night in a darkened
room.

Two candles give the only illumination . . . The windows
are shrouded and all sources of light masked. At the top
of the room is a table draped with the South African flag.
As a symbol of Afrikaner exclusivity and rejection of the
British . . . the Union Jack in the flag is covered.

   There is a flickering candle at each end of the table.
Standing behind it is the Broeder who will conduct
the induction ceremony, usually the chairman of the
branch. The recruit is escorted into the room by his
sponsors and stands facing the table. Silently, the
branch members – who are not known by him to be
Broeders – file into the room and stand, unseen, behind
him. Those who will contribute to the ceremony have
torches to read their passages from the induction hand-
book. Now the emotional and psychological preparation
for the induction begins.

Sometimes there is a hymn. Always there is a Scripture
reading and a prayer, and a call from the chairman that 'in
these moments of deep seriousness' the other Broeders
should recall their own induction ceremony and reaffirm
their vows.

The recruit, always referred to by his full name, is then addressed by the chairman who tells him the conditions of membership and asks him to 'solemnly declare' that he is not a member of any other secret organisation and that he will not reveal anything about the Broederbond that he learns that night. Having received the promise of the recruit, he goes on to read the raison d'être of the organisation:

The Afrikaner Broederbond is born from a deep conviction that the Afrikaner nation, with its own characteristics and destiny, was placed in this country by God the Three-in-One, and that this nation has been called to remain in existence as long as it pleases God.

The members of the Afrikaner Broederbond are Afrikaners, aware of their calling, who strive to live out the best in our nation, and to serve.

The Afrikaner Broederbond is wholly devoted to the service of the Afrikaner nation and does not exist to serve or promote the personal interests of its members. Those who join do so to give, not to receive; to serve, not to be served or personally advantaged.

On the basis of our belief in God, and in His service and honour, the Afrikaner Broederbond aims to unite its members in a strong bond of mutual trust and love of their nation; to bind them in love, despite their differences; to work selflessly for the establishment of a healthy common purpose among all Afrikaners who strive for the welfare and advancement of all interests of the Afrikaner nation.

Because membership of the Afrikaner Broederbond entails great responsibility, it is necessary that you carefully consider what will be expected of you. Therefore, I call upon a number of experienced Broeders to inform you about this.

Two Broeders then take it in turns to read aloud the things expected of the new member, many of them sounding for all the world like something out of the Boy Scouts' manual.

'It will be expected of you that you will steadfastly fulfil your duties as a member and that you will faithfully attend the monthly branch meetings.'

'It will be expected of you that you will at all times in your behaviour uphold the honour, value and good name of the Afrikaner Broederbond.'

The chairman ends a list of similar expectations with the words: 'Brotherhood demands of you work and rugged perseverance. At times it demands conflict and unpleasantness. It not only demands the combating of that which is evil, but more especially obedience to and the practice of Christian principles.'

When the recruit has said that he understands and complies with all of this, he is asked to 'solemnly undertake' five promises which involve swearing never to reveal his own or anyone else's membership of the Broederbond, or revealing anything that takes place in the Broederbond and to be subject to the conditions of the constitution which include 'immediate expulsion' if he breaks any of them.

The recruit is then given a few moments' silence to reflect on the enormity of these promises before he is asked to give his pledge. Once given, the chairman winds up the ceremony with the words:

In the name of the Afrikaner Broederbond, and in the presence of the other Broeders who stand here as witnesses of the irrevocable union you have forged, I accept your promise of faith and declare you a Broeder.

In the words of our motto, I wish you strength.
Be strong in the practice of your brotherhood.
Be strong in faith if the struggle becomes onerous.
Be strong in your love of your nation.
Be strong in the service of your nation.

With a hearty handshake I, and after that the other Broeders, want to assure you that we accept you from now on as a fellow Broeder.
Hearty congratulations and welcome.

The lights are then turned on. The new Broeder looks into the faces of his new brothers, many of whom he may have known and worked with for years and he pays his R40.

Nico felt instantly ill at ease. If he had thought for one moment that the vows and stated intentions revealed at the initiation ceremony were fairly harmless, if somewhat childish, his first monthly meeting soon dispelled any illusions. Straightaway, he got a glimpse of the ruthlessness of the Afrikaner Broederbond.

The meeting was discussing the behaviour of a local Afrikaner postmaster who would not co-operate by allowing a member of the Broederbond to get a telephone early and thus jump the queue. The postmaster said he must wait his turn, like the rest of the community.

But the Broederbond decided this man was not a true Afrikaner and was not promoting the interests of the Afrikaners. They would discuss the matter with the Minister of Telecommunications. As a result, the postmaster was removed. He was uprooted from his home and community and sent to another post office in another area.

'I was shocked,' recalls Nico, 'I was so upset. I thought this is not a service to the Afrikaner community. You can justify all sorts of evil actions under the guise of "service". And are the Afrikaner people of so much importance that you must promote their interest above all others?'

He went back that night and told Ellen he had made a terrible mistake. She was too much of a friend to say 'I told you so.'

*   *   *

Mistake or not, it was the Broederbond that got him his next, and most influential, position. Nico had been working as mission secretary for three years, and still saw himself primarily as a missionary, though he had started work on his doctorate in an attempt to catch up with his academic work – badly neglected during his time at Venda.

When the University of Stellenbosch – perhaps the most prestigious of all Afrikaner universities – invited him to become their senior lecturer in missiology, Nico had no doubt at all that it was the work of the Broederbond. He

knew several other men who were eligible for the job, and
all of them were more highly qualified than he. None of
them was a Broeder. It was clear that the Brotherhood
wanted their own man in this influential position.

Nico couldn't accept. He felt it would be immoral to take
a job that other men were clearly more capable of filling.
And yet something told him he could not reject it out of
hand. He struggled and struggled until the day before his
decision had to be made.

He and Ellen and their children had planned a boat trip
to Beira, and ringing the university authorities he asked
for one more week's grace, hoping that the sea voyage
would clear his mind and give him the confidence to make
the right decision.

It certainly did, though not in the manner he had
envisaged.

On the return trip from Beira to Durban their little ship
was caught up in a terrible typhoon. For three days they
thrashed around at sea. All the passengers were confined
to their bunks as forty-foot waves crashed over the vessel.
The sound of the wind and the cracking of the ship was
terrifying. Nico and Ellen did their best to stay calm for
the sake of the children, but they really felt that there was
little chance of survival.

'I kept thinking about Jonah! I felt in my heart that God
wanted me to go to Stellenbosch, but I couldn't bring
myself to say "Yes, Lord," because I was so aware that I
was not qualified or capable enough to do the job. But I was
so terrified I eventually said, "Lord, if we come out of this
typhoon alive, I'll go."'

When they finally touched dry land, very shaken by the
experience, Nico phoned the university and fixed an
appointment with the secretary of the curatorium.

'He was not a member of the Broederbond, I knew that,
and he was a wise man. I spoke very openly with him and
he said that it was true that I had been called because of
my membership of the Broederbond, and not because of
my qualifications. He said it had been very clear that the
appointment had been organised beforehand, because
when it came to the vote I was immediately elected,

despite the fact that there were several candidates who were obviously more suitable. Then he was silent for quite a long time, looking at the ground. "But in spite of all this," he said, "I believe it is right."'

Later, when Nico publicly renounced the Broederbond and embarrassed the university establishment, this man was to prove his protector and friend. The Broederbond, however, lived to rue the day they had manipulated Nico into the faculty of theology, and Ellen's mother, who had been living with them for three years (and quietly driving them mad), was furious with Nico for taking her daughter so far away, and went into another depression from which she did not emerge until three months before her death.

14

THE PAIN OF BEING WRONG

Stellenbosch is beautiful. A fool's paradise. As you stroll through the dappled streets, hearing only the wood-doves, seeing the lovely bright shadows of a winter afternoon, you would never believe that there was any such thing as a black man, or that the country was in the throes of a bloody, civil war.

The old Cape houses, graceful and solid, gleam brilliant white in the sun. The gardens are thick with magnolia and bougainvillaea and the trees grow tall, laced with morning glory and the little black-eyed Susan. There is an attractive maturity about the town, protected as it is by tall mountains beneath a cloudless winter sky.

The maid who stands at the gate in her pink uniform and starched white apron will be coloured. The gardener also, and they live in their own part of town – a dishevelled area of badly-constructed houses, lumped together in what looks like a corporation tip.

The Smiths, on the other hand, built a beautiful house in Van der Stel Street, and settled down to relish their new life. They bought bicycles and would cycle out as a family to explore their new environment. In the early days Nico was on the school committee and organised the family games for the kids and their parents. They relished the antiquity of the town and the richness of their social and intellectual life.

But slowly, imperceptibly at first, the parents began to withdraw from family activities as the demands of their own lives grew. Ellen decided she wanted to leave general medicine and study psychology. She first had to get her BSc degree, then an honours degree, then her MA. It took

her five years of hard slog, and she got distinctions in all
of them. The university offered her a lectureship in psychology. (Unkind colleagues used to say, 'Ellen had the
brains and Nico had the Broederbond.')

But after three years' lecturing, and eight out of general
medicine, she began to miss the contact with patients. She
felt that psychology was just verbal therapy. She didn't
really know enough about treatment, and too many of the
cases she saw were real psychiatric cases, but she couldn't
prescribe. So she decided to turn to psychiatry. That
meant another four years' study. And that was hard. She
began at 7.30 each morning in the wards, attended lectures during the day, and saw her own patients.

The children would come home from school to find one
patient sitting in the sitting room, another in the dining
room, and a third on the veranda while their mother was
dealing with a fourth in her study.

Sometimes patients would be given a bed for the night if
it was too late to admit them to hospital. The children
would be woken up to the sounds of a stranger wandering
around the house and they'd all leap out of bed to placate
whoever it was and put them back to sleep.

Although officially home each afternoon, Ellen was
always absorbed in her work or her patients, and there
was a continual flow of visitors to Nico's study in which
he held court to lecturers and students and visiting
academics.

Teenagers now, the girls resented the fact that their
home was never their own, that their parents were always
busy. They found it painful to discover that they came
second to an ideal. The vision both parents had for their
work appeared to take priority over family life.

They accused their father of having to make an appointment with him if they wanted to talk. They told him they
never saw their mother, that she never had any time to be
with them and he'd say, well, she's at home in the afternoons. And so she was, but usually with an entourage of
the mentally sick.

In fact the parents were so busy that the children felt
almost unloved. There never seemed to be any time for

them, no space for them to discuss their problems, or just the everyday things of life. 'Mum, can I go to a party?' would be met with, 'I'm too busy to discuss that now, we'll wait and see,' so the children wouldn't know until the day if they were able to go.

Because Nico and Ellen were so taken up with the problems of others and the demands of their own professional lives, they seemed to have no energy left to deal with the needs of those closest to them. One daughter recalls clearly the stresses of those days. The whole family had been to Europe for nine months' sabbatical and the children had to make up the schoolwork they'd missed while away concurrently with the year they were doing. She became distraught with the pressure and one day said to Ellen, 'Mum I really must talk to you,' and Ellen replied, 'Can't you see that I'm exhausted. Why do you have to come to me with your troubles now?'

But during the first ten years of their time in Stellenbosch, Nico was going through his own traumas. And it was the Broederbond that triggered them off. The question posed by Karl Barth had never left him, and the more he knew about the Broederbond, attending their meetings and listening to their discussions, the more aware he became that he was not free.

The Broederbond activities were completely focused on the Afrikaner people and their interests and he began to ask himself if they were justified in thinking so much about the Afrikaner, and if it really was necessary for them to rule the country. It had the effect of turning his eyes away from his own people to the Africans and coloureds.

'We had many coloureds in Stellenbosch and I was aware that they spoke the same language, Afrikaans, and had the same culture and history. And I thought how could I possibly not accept them? How could I say that they must not participate in our world, when they were a part of our world?'

And so Nico began to enter a painful and confusing time of re-evaluation. It was partly painful because he knew that if he ever voiced his reservations about the accepted place of blacks in society and the role of the Afrikaner, his friends and colleagues would regard him with grave suspicion and doubt. To be thought of as a liberal, a radical, was a very terrible thing in his society and he had no desire to be thought of as a very terrible thing.

But there was one man to whom he could speak his doubts openly, Professor Johannes Degenaar who, with his wife Jetti, lived over the road.

Every now and then you meet someone in your life who sets you free. It's a rare and precious experience. You find the parameters of your understanding widened. You are not afraid to explore old taboos, to re-evaluate long-held concepts. New possibilities of other explanations open up to you, and far from being afraid, you feel an unexpected freedom, a liberation, from a prison you never realised you were in.

Such is the experience even a few hours' conversation with Johannes Degenaar can bring. There is a gentleness about him. You do not sense that he wants to destroy or to threaten you. He does not blame you for what you think, or reject you however profoundly he disagrees. But he will not cease to challenge you if he feels that you are wrong, continually asking you, 'What do you mean by that? What exactly do you mean?'

As a young man, Degenaar had been the first professor at Stellenbosch to break away from the Afrikaner establishment and openly attack apartheid. Highly articulate and intelligent, he was, and is, light years away from most of his colleagues, and he was a constant source of grievance to the authorities.

Unlike Nico, he wasn't answerable to the Church, and his position as professor of philosophy meant that he couldn't just be thrown out for his views. When things got too hot, he buried his head in his books and waited for the storm to blow over, and that way he survived.

Degenaar was known as a rebel and he gathered around him a small group of radical thinkers who met every month to formulate their opinions and to discuss current issues. No one could have been better suited to lead Nico through the painful process of his spiritual and theological evolution, and that is what he did. He and Jetti became, in the end, the life support for Nico and Ellen as they struggled with a new understanding.

In re-evaluating his position, Nico had to start from where he first began, believing that apartheid was Biblically justifiable and for the good of all.

My mind was so much infected by the whole concept that separation was right, that I couldn't see that it was really damaging, that it was violating people. It was too deeply ingrained in me that separation was for their benefit. That was the main heresy I kept battling away with, that separation was for their own benefit.

I wasn't challenged by their poverty, or by the menial positions they held because I knew too little about their real circumstances. I don't think privileged people ever think sensitively about the poverty of others. They assume that they are poor because they're inferior in some way, or that they're not civilised, not socially mature.

But as, ironically, the activities of the Broederbond turned his attention away from the Afrikaner, he began to worry, and to search the Scriptures for new answers.

First there was the verse in Colossians (1:4) where Paul says, 'we have heard . . . of your love for all God's people'. What puzzled Nico was that Paul could say for *all* God's people.

'I couldn't say that. I asked myself, can I really say I love God's people even when they're black? No. I couldn't. I didn't have any real feeling for them.'

Then he turned up the verses in 2 Corinthians 5 where Paul says that he no longer judged people by human standards, and Nico realised that unless you look at people with eyes that have first seen the cross, you cannot see their true value in God's eyes. He began to re-evaluate his fellow human beings, whatever their colour, viewing them not with his natural human instincts, but through the eye of a God who had died for them.

I began to realise that if the other person, like me, was also made in the image of God, and if God valued them so highly that he sent his son to die for them, I could not possibly send them away, just push them aside, which is what separation means in practice. I had to become involved with them. I could not say they had less of God's image in them and I more! And I realised it was sheer aggression to tell a person that because they were black they could not come into my church, could not be part of my world. Through Christ we were now part of each other's world and could not be separated.

Working on a study of Ephesians emphasised the point. Here Paul explained that God was calling into existence a whole new humanity through Christ. A divine humanity. A humanity in which the old divisions were done away with, in which all mankind was bound together into one body by Christ's death on the cross. Paul wrote:

By means of the cross he [Christ] united both races into one body and brought them back to God. It is through Christ that all of us . . . are able to come in the one Spirit into the presence of the Father . . .

There is one body and one Spirit, just as there is one hope to which God has called you. There is one Lord, one faith, one baptism; there is one God and Father of all mankind, who is Lord of all, works through all, and is in all.

Paul went on:

Your hearts and minds must be made completely new, and you must put on the new self, which is created in God's likeness . . . Do not use harmful words, but only helpful words, the kind that build up and provide what is needed . . . Get rid of all bitterness, passion and anger. No more shouting or insults, no more hateful feelings of any sort. Instead, be kind and tender-hearted to one another . . . Your life must be controlled by love.

Was Nico's life controlled by love? Were his attitudes to blacks and coloureds kind and tender-hearted? Were his mind and heart 'completely new'? He came to see that the answer to all these questions was no. His attitude to blacks had not been governed by Biblical principles at all, but by a strong sense of national identity and a fear that if the races intermingled that identity, which was his identity, would be threatened. He had never made the essential switch from feeling he belonged to a human nation to realising he belonged to a new spiritual nation in which there was neither Greek nor Jew, slave nor free, but one people united in Christ.

There was a long time when he could not reconcile himself with what he was beginning to understand. It was a period of confusion and anxiety. He would talk it over with Ellen, but while she was sympathetic, she could see that it was eating him up, and felt he was becoming obsessed with this internal struggle. He was getting it out of proportion.

His searching at this time led him to ask a very fundamental question; how did the West develop its ruler mentality in the first place?

President Kaunda once said that the difference between Western people and black people was that Westerners had an aggressive problem-solving mind, and Africans had a mind that 'experienced' situations.

Nico illustrates this by talking about the Western approach to meeting, which is to launch immediately into the business, finish as quickly as possible, and disperse. The African will take time asking about his colleague's welfare, his family, his personal situation. Time will be spent just being together, experiencing one another.

'Because we are,' says African philosophy, 'therefore I am.' They have evolved a 'belonging' culture, as opposed to the 'doing' culture of the West expounded by Descartes who said, 'I think, therefore I am.' The African would argue, 'I belong, therefore I am'. What Kaunda said caught Nico's attention. He knew immediately that he was describing his own problem.

As I began to experience a closer contact with African people I became aware of a very dominating aspect in my own personality. It was almost a subconscious thing, but I found that I automatically wanted to dominate them. It was as if I was saying that I knew the right way to do things and they just had to accept that I was right. That my perspectives were right. And this was the way forwards.

When I discovered how bad, how evil that was, I began to look into my own personality to discover the roots of such an attitude. I came to realise that it wasn't just me, but that I was part of a whole civilisation that had developed an arrogant and aggressive attitude, a ruler mentality that sought to dominate and rode roughshod over the sensibilities and perceptions of everybody who held a different point of view.

There were two articles that set Nico thinking. The first was by an Austrian theologian who pointed out how Western man, since the early Middle Ages, began to develop this aggressive mentality which became tied up with the whole Christian movement.

It really started way back with Constantine the Great who was, in one sense, the first 'Christian' ruler. When he, as Emperor of Rome, became converted to Christianity, Christianity became an acceptable faith for the first time in its history, and he eventually made it the only legal religion of the Roman Empire. Christian rulers came to believe that wherever they moved, they must proselytise. Colonising and Christianising became part of the same parcel. As you conquered, you converted.

The Middle Ages in Europe were times of great expansion and colonisation, much of it done in the name of 'Christianity'. The Europeans felt themselves to be a superior people, and part of their superiority lay in their Christianity which they imposed with impunity on whomsoever they conquered.

The second article Nico read was by Professor Berkhof, who developed the argument further. He posed the question: how could Western Christianity have developed such a triumphant, conquering attitude when it preached Jesus as the incarnate son of God, coming to this world as a servant and not as a king? How could Western Christianity have adopted such an aggressive attitude to fellow human beings when their 'role model' was the Son of God who lived among the poor and rejected, and who took a towel and washed his disciples' feet?

Nico says:

It was a revelation to me. I discovered that as Westerners we Afrikaners had come to a continent where the people put all their emphasis on being human. To the African, a person is a person for another person. You are only a person through another person. It's very deep. They believe you can't just think in terms of yourself. That your very identity is dependent upon the identity of the other. That your well-being is dependent on his or her well-being.

And so there we were, we Westerners, we came to South Africa and we said; these people are barbarians, they're heathens, they don't know anything. We must Christianise them. We have to be the masters, we are responsible under God for developing this country and for helping them to develop acceptable Christian attitudes.

The most painful and harmful thing one person can do to another person is not to accept him or her. As people we need other people not only to survive but for our fulfilment as a human being. We were created like this, that is what it means to be human. We all need to feel that we have a certain worth as people and whenever we do not get that assurance, especially from those near to us, it causes loneliness.

Loneliness, in its essence, means that I am denied as a person. My existence is denied and this is what hurts.

Our humanity means community; acceptance of one another. This is why it is so painful that we, as Westerners and whites, being in authority in this country, have created a system of separation, because the policy of separation, to the African people, is saying to them, 'You're not wanted. We don't like you and don't want you near to us.' And that is why, to the African people, the policy of apartheid is so inhuman.

I have heard so many of them ask how South Africa can ever say that it is a Christian country when they are exercising the most unChristian and inhuman system possible. That is how they understand our system, our society. Our presence on this continent is seen as being inhuman. We are a group of people not willing to have community, fellowship, contact and communication.

So Nico came to understand that the result of separation was the degradation of human beings. Black people in white South Africa were reduced to functions. The moment they had no function they were not wanted or allowed.

He discovered one clause in the legislation which says that 'jobless and superfluous' black people could be removed by the authorities to other parts of the country they called 'homelands'.

'They are resettled in areas where they are out of sight and out of mind, and we just carry on enjoying our privileges without caring what happens to them as people.'

The state's insistence that the National Party has a Christian base, and that as whites they have the responsibility of 'maintaining civilised standards and Christian norms' (as President Botha would say) fills Nico with shame.

'Even if the politicians are too insensitive to understand the profound truths of the African philosophy, why can't they, as politicians and as alleged Christians, have a servant attitude? Why don't they realise that they are here in the first place to serve the people, not to be their rulers?'

Nico also came to see it as a sign of deep corruption in the whites that they cannot believe that the blacks have not only the morality to govern the country, but the compassion to treat the whites with sensitivity. The very fear the whites express for their own future he sees as a reflection of their own immorality.

'Because they themselves do not care what happens to the blacks, they cannot understand that perhaps the blacks do care what happens to them. That the blacks still have the humanity to care what happens to other human beings. Power has so corrupted the whites here that they cannot believe that black people can be human enough to want the whites also to have a quality of life.'

A black colleague of Nico's described it like this:

Maybe the whites are not human enough to see me as a human being. Maybe they speak like that blind man who, after Christ touched his eyes and asked him what he could see, said, 'I see people like trees that are walking.'

Maybe we blacks are seen as trees, and maybe we are oppressed like trees; we have to yield fruit, we have to labour for their good.

But black theology emphasises that it is vital to love the oppressor and to care as much for his redemption, as for the freedom of those they oppress.

The Kairos Document, published in 1985 by a group of prominent black and white theologians, made the same point:

. . . The oppressor and those who believe the propaganda of the oppressor are desperately fearful. They must be made aware of the diabolical evils of the present system and they must be called to repentance . . .

But they must also be given something to hope for. At present they have false hopes. They hope to maintain the status quo and their special privileges with perhaps some adjustments and they fear any real alternative. But there is much more than that to hope for and nothing to fear. Can the Christian message of hope not help them in this matter?

For Nico, the revelation that all his life he had been acting like a ruler, and not like a servant, led to a fundamental change in his attitude not only to blacks, but to himself and his role in society.

> I came to see that I must really be willing to be a servant of the people. That no matter what I think needs to be done in South Africa, I should not try to motivate people to do it my way, but just be part of them and think through with them, a way in which a new future can be created.
>
> As an Afrikaner I must not think: 'How can the minorities be protected? How can I safeguard myself against possible atrocities? How can my own culture be protected?' Instead I must think: 'How can I really serve the country and all its people?' And I need to work this out with fellow blacks.

On an international scale Nico would attribute the failure of communities like the United Nations and the EEC to be really effective reconcilers to this 'ruler mentality'.

> They don't work as well as they should because contributing countries are still thinking: what can I get out of it? And not: how can I serve humanity through it?
>
> Those that do have an idealistic view of what these organisations could achieve are regarded as naïve because most people say such a concept cannot work in politics. In politics you have to rule and to get the best out of every situation for yourself and your own people, and never mind everybody else.

To Nico the tragedy is that in this respect, Christianity has failed.

> Much that is good in the world has been developed through Christian initiative, but we've missed out on the one essential ingredient of Christianity, that of being servants to one another.
>
> World history would have been so different if only we had understood and obeyed. If only we had taken a towel instead of a sword.

15

SOCIAL SUICIDE

Ellen constantly urged Nico to leave the Broederbond, but
he was afraid. He knew what the consequences would be.
To leave the Brotherhood would be social suicide. He was a
well-known man, a well-respected man. He was a popular
guest speaker, a figure of consequence. Once a Brother left
the Broederbond a directive went round every member
that he was to be cut off from all meaningful communication. If Nico left he would be dubbed a traitor and
ostracised by friends and colleagues. He would be socially
and academically ignored, a leper among his own people.

What is more, the chair was about to fall vacant, but
what chance would he have of becoming professor if he
publicly renounced the very men who had his appointment in their power? His academic life would be in ruins.
Nico didn't know if he had the courage to face such
awesome consequences.

And yet he saw more clearly than ever the evils of an
ideology.

I realised that the real evil of an ideology was that it
tried to protect people from reality and make them
believe in a utopia that was possible if they only believed and acted in a certain way. In this utopia they
would be happy. Most ideologies are out to promote the
good life for those who believe in them, without suffering or sacrifice on their part.

That is not Christianity. Our aim is not to be happy.
Christianity is out to promote a good life for the other
person. And we expect suffering to be part of our experience. We say that as Christians we must be willing

to be a servant and not a lord. It is by becoming a
servant that you find the deepest meaning of life and
of love.

It took Nico the best part of eight years to reach this point,
where he could say at last that he was truly free from the
ideology of his past and prepared to face the consequences
of his future. In his heart he had made the transition from
master to slave. It now remained for him to make a public
break with his past and all that he had renounced, and his
opportunity came in the spring of 1973.

There was at this time a big political upheaval in the
National Party. Trouble had been brewing for some years
between the ultra right-wing followers of Dr Albert Hertzog and the rest of the Broederbond and National Party. It
reached such a pitch that in 1969 Hertzog was forced out
of the party and formed the HNP (Herstige Nasionale
Party). It's a long and tedious story of intrigue and
power seeking, but the result was a Broederbond divided
sharply between the 'Verligtes' (the enlightened) and the
'Verkrampte' (ultra right-wingers). Acting on the idiom
that united we stand, divided we fall, the Broederbond,
and indeed the current Prime Minister, Mr Vorster, knew
that a divided Afrikanerdom was a weak Afrikanerdom,
and that it was of the utmost importance to restore
unity.

Vorster also knew that without the support of the
Broederbond, no Nationalist could ever become Prime
Minister, let alone rule the country effectively. If they
wanted to stay in control, the schism in the Bond had to be
healed.

One of the measures they took was to hold an extraordinary meeting at all branches of the Bond at which
every member had to rededicate himself to the Brotherhood and reaffirm his loyalty to the National Party, swearing that they had no connection with the HNP. Branches
were instructed that all members had to attend and that
the meeting should be conducted in a solemn atmosphere
and opened with Scripture and prayer. The induction
pledge had to be read to the members followed by a two-

minute silence during which they should consider their
position before signing.

The exercise turned out to be a triumph for the Broederbond and for Vorster. Of the 9,027 members, 8,859 signed.
The hold of the HNP was effectively broken and the threat
of Dr Hertzog and his cronies removed.

But to those men, like Nico, who had reservations about
the Broederbond, this was an opportunity to get out. Many
individuals left the Broederbond at this stage and faded
quietly into the background of national life.

The difference with Nico, as his colleagues and former
Broeders acidly remarked, was that he always did things
more publicly than anyone else! He hadn't attended that
crucial meeting intending to leave. It just turned out that
way.

He had been phoned that morning, along with all the
other members of his cell, and instructed that there was an
urgent meeting that night at which they would be asked
to sign a document saying they were reaffirming their
loyalty to the Broederbond and the National Party.

Nico was unhappy about it, and he told them so. 'You've
always told me that we were not political, we were just
a cultural organisation. Now we are being asked to pledge
loyalty to the National Party. Is that a cultural organisation?'

For three hours his fellow Broeders argued about
whether they were really cultural or political and in the
end Nico said he could not sign. At first they tried to tell
him not to take it all so seriously, but he was adamant.

When the Dean of the Faculty, who was a staunch
Broeder, discovered that Nico had left, he warned him not
to say anything against the Broederbond or the Party.
'Just keep quiet for a couple of years and they'll forget all
about you,' he said, 'but if you start speaking out they'll
give you a very hard time.'

Keeping quiet is not part of Nico's nature. He lay low for
nearly a year, but could contain himself no longer. He
launched into a series of public statements that left not
only his fellow Broeders in no doubt about his point of
view, but the rest of South Africa as well. The next six

years were to be a contentious time during which most of
his worst fears came true.

He quickly became persona non grata among the intel-
ligentsia of Stellenbosch. His views were considered
dangerous and nobody wanted to hear him any more. He
was no longer asked to do visiting lectures, or called to run
missionary weekends. He was socially ignored and per-
petually harassed by the university authorities who put
his every word and action under a microscope. Student
members of the junior Broederbond were instructed to
report on the content of his lectures and if he was felt
to be getting too near the bone, he was hauled in front of
the 'big boys' and called to order. Some subjects they forbade him to speak about, not because they were unrelated
to his lectures, but because they were 'confusing the
students'.

Time and time again he was called before the Curatorium, which is the disciplinary body of the faculty of
theology, to answer for his actions, to account for his time,
to be cross-examined on his teaching, his conversations,
his attitudes. They tried everything they knew to under-
mine his authority with the students and to knock his
self-esteem.

But Nico's initial reaction at finally making the break
with the Broederbond was one of profound relief. He went
home to Ellen and said, 'Now I am free.'

'I felt an enormous sense of liberation knowing that I
was no longer forced to think how the group was thinking.
I was free to speak out the Gospel as I understood it. I no
longer felt I needed to be careful, that I mustn't upset
people. I was at last free.'

Nevertheless, to be 'demoted' to a nobody in his professional and social life was hard to take. Even more bitter,
perhaps, was the attitude of his friends. Charles Fensham,
also a professor and his friend since childhood, had visited
Nico and Ellen almost every week for the last eight years,
but once Nico left the Broederbond Charles no longer
called. 'He became a complete stranger to me. We never
saw him again except at social functions and then he was
very cold and impersonal.'

Nico recalled that at the time of his most public utter-
ings against the Pretoria régime, Charles would write
scathing, but anonymous letters about him in the press.
He knew they were from Charles because he recognised
his style, but he also knew that Charles didn't want to sign
them out of respect for their years of friendship.

But there was one pleasant surprise in store for Nico.
Despite his leaving the Broederbond, he was still elected
for the chair of missiology.

Why, he's still not clear, except that God was obviously
at work. But at the time he felt that because the chair
always went to the senior lecturer, it would be too obvious
to the whole world that he was not being appointed because he had left the Broederbond. The Brotherhood were
not prepared to reveal that sort of immorality to public
view. But it was a near thing. He was elected by a majority
of one vote.

Nico now felt free to express in public the anxieties that
he had been wrestling with for so long in private, and
his status as professor gave considerable weight to his
arguments.

His first attack appeared in *Die Burger* newspaper when
he accused the Dutch Reformed Church of being so involved with the Afrikaner *Volk* and their national identity that they were not free to preach the true Gospel to all
people. It caused a howl of rage in the press and ignited the
faculty of theology. The one thing that Afrikanerdom is
extremely touchy about is its morality. To suggest for one
moment that Afrikaners were not acting in a completely
moral way, according to their perspective of morality, was
to cause deep offence and had the Church and political
leadership jumping up and down in agitation.

Nico was summoned to the curatorium to answer for his
opinions. It was the first time that he had been called to
account, and not knowing quite what to expect, he was
filled with apprehension.

I lay awake at night before the meeting wondering what
they were going to say. What would they do? Would they
chuck me out? I had a real fear of confrontation and I

would get terribly upset trying to work things out in my own mind. Maybe I was wrong after all. Maybe I shouldn't have said what I did.

And then I would think no, I can't be wrong and I'd pray, 'Dear Lord, just help me to be willing to stand and say what I think.' But it was hell. I could feel it in my stomach. I really feared rejection.

When he entered the room for the confrontation there were six people present, including the Secretary of the Curatorium and the Dean of the Faculty. They immediately launched into the attack, reading out loud to him the things that had been written in the press.

They were not interested in what Nico had to say. They were not interested in the content of his arguments, they were concerned only about the image of the faculty which they felt would be damaged by this type of controversy. They were also concerned lest Nico's ideas should influence the students. They made all this abundantly clear to him, trying their best to make him feel like a naughty boy who had been hauled up before the headmaster for a smack. It was to be the first of many such meetings.

The dust had not long settled on this public furore when he caused another, this time on the Day of Pentecost. All professors had to preach two public sermons a year, and this being Pentecost, Nico preached about the Holy Spirit being the spirit that brought unity, binding all peoples together in Christ.

He challenged the congregation to invite the members of the coloured church, who met just five hundred metres down the road, to tea and sandwiches in the church hall, so that they could demonstrate their oneness in Christ. Nico spoke with all the new-found conviction of his heart, and the congregation received his sermon in a profound silence.

'I heard the next day that two families had written to the church council protesting that I had used the pulpit as a political platform, and they wanted me to answer for it.'

It was, of course, the tea and sandwiches that had

caused the upset, and Nico quite thought the church council would just forget all about it. Not a bit of it. A commission was appointed to talk to the complainants and to Nico. The families said they would drop the matter only if Nico made a public apology on the front page of the church's quarterly magazine. Nico naturally replied that he could do no such thing. He wasn't going to apologise for the Gospel.

One of the members of the commission happened to be a colleague at the university, a fine gentleman.

He came to my study and said in his very formal way, 'Now, colleague, be realistic. You were saying that we must invite the coloured church council and members to have tea together, but can't you understand that some of the people in that congregation over the street are the farm labourers on our own members' farms. How can you expect a labourer to drink tea with the owner?'

I said, 'Colleague, that is exactly what I expect. That is what the Church is. On the farm one may be the owner, the other the servant, but in the Church of God they are brothers. Having tea together would be an expression of the work of the Holy Spirit in their lives.'

He gave up on me. Said he couldn't see my point at all, and couldn't I try to be realistic.

The argument carried on for nine months, and then eventually fizzled out, but not before Nico was called for the second time to stand before the curatorium.

As usual they did not address the issue at hand. They did not discuss the rights and wrongs of what Nico was saying, but only the possible repercussions. If people thought that the DRC was criticising the Afrikaner people, or thought there was any sort of disturbance in the Church, they would stop sending their students to the theological faculty and financial contributions would dry up.

Nico must realise that he was in a very responsible position and had to be careful what he expressed publicly.

They expected him to be more circumspect from now on.

'Well,' said Nico, 'I can't promise you that. My conscience must be free.'

*   *   *

Professor Sampie Terreblanche is a man of such intellectual and emotional enthusiasm, and waves his arms around with such vigour, that you quite expect to be bespattered with shirt buttons. He has the charisma of a born teacher so that even those of us who are unable to add up on our fingers and toes sit spellbound as he expounds his economic theories on the survival, or possibly the non-survival, of South Africa.

He describes himself disarmingly as a 'Johnny-come-lately' and is now following in Nico's footsteps, if a few miles behind. But in the days when Nico was opposing the Broederbond from the hallowed precincts of the faculty of theology, Sampie Terreblanche found him far from endearing.

'Our circle was frankly antagonistic towards him. He and I had been friends. When he was in the Broederbond there was a relationship of confidence between us. We talked freely. When he left the Broederbond all that was lost. The atmosphere changed between us. For a time we were sharp enemies.'

One of the main bones of contention was Nico's insistence that so-called cultural organisations – of which the Broederbond billed itself as one – were a stumbling-block to change. Everyone was talking about 'change', but rigorously clinging to these old organisations which still believed that the Afrikaner must maintain his identity at all costs. What sort of change, he argued, could come out of that?

While he never mentioned the Broederbond by name, they felt his criticisms were aimed at them and they were filled with righteous indignation. They were going through quite a radical internal crisis at the time and there is no doubt that the *Verligtes* among them were fighting for radical reforms. Charles Fensham was one of those who supported a four-chamber parliament which included urban blacks, and was bitterly disappointed when the idea was thrown out.

But Nico's point was this: even if the Broederbond did want change, it was a change they considered best. They did not consult the blacks about it. They said they wanted a more open society, where all but the very basic laws of apartheid – the Group Areas Act and the Race Classification Act – were abolished, but they were not willing to consult with the blacks, or go so far as to say that the country needed a completely new political dispensation in which the blacks would have a meaningful participation in politics.

'I felt they were still an exclusive group, keeping power in their own hands, still manipulating. They were like the colonisers, believing they knew best, and that they had the right to dictate to the blacks what changes should take place.'

Tension between Nico and the Broederbond grew so great that one afternoon he received a phone call to say that Sampie Terreblanche and another professor wanted to call on him that evening. 'I wondered why, all of a sudden, they should want to see me!'

When they called, fairly late in the evening, it was clear to Nico that the Bond had sent them to warn him off. 'I was shocked. They said they'd had enough of my trying to insinuate that the Broederbond was a hindrance to change and that they were indoctrinating the people and they wanted me to know that if I didn't stop talking against the Broederbond I'd be in trouble. They were actually trying to intimidate me. I couldn't believe it.'

'Now,' says Sampie Terreblanche, 'I have to say that Nico was so often correct. But at the time we attacked him like hell.'

And hell it was for Nico. The tentacles of the Broederbond were everywhere. On one occasion he got a couple of days' academic leave to visit his students in Pretoria to talk over the doctorates. At that time Beyers Naudé was still under house arrest and only allowed one visitor at a time. Nico rang him – it was a long time since they'd met –

and made an appointment to call at Beyers' home the following day.

Nico had made the phone call in the evening. Early the next morning the telephone wires between Stellenbosch and Pretoria were humming as the Rector of the university rang round all Nico's friends and colleagues leaving urgent messages for him to ring back immediately. Having finally tracked Nico down, the Rector asked him what on earth he was doing in Pretoria. Furious, Nico refused to talk to him on the phone and said he'd call at the Rector's office when he got back.

For once Nico was on the attack. He was horrified, not only that the Rector should ring a professor and ask him to account for himself in that way, but that the Broederbond – because that's who it was – could have such widespread power and influence.

The secret police tapped Beyers' phone, but Nico assumes they must have tipped off the Rector to inform him of his movements. Any contact with Beyers Naudé would have been regarded as very dangerous by the Afrikaner establishment.

Nico pushed the Rector to tell him how he had been informed, but the Rector refused to answer. All he would say was that as Rector it was his responsibility to keep an eye on the staff and he had been told that some lecturers were asking for academic leave and spending the time on the beach 'lying in the sun all day'. He was just making sure that Nico's trip was bona fide.

It was not long after that that Nico and Ellen discovered that a tap had been put on their own phone. One of the students who had been challenged by some of Nico's lectures came in tears to him one day to say that the security police had recruited him to inform on Nico, and to report back the contents of his lectures. He bitterly regretted it and was not going to be used by the police again, but he wanted to warn Nico to be careful because his phone had been tapped.

However bouyant Nico appeared before his colleagues and the Curatorium, it actually devastated him inside. If they wanted to make his life a misery, they were succeeding. There was something very wearing about this continuous scrutiny, the fact that they were on his back all the time.

It was a calculated intimidation, and they were trying to break him down. Often he would cry out, 'Lord, must I really say this? Can't I keep quiet this once? Allow me to keep quiet and just enjoy my position here.'

In his study there hung a copy of Rembrandt's picture of Jeremiah. Nico used to look at the prophet sitting there as if the world was coming down upon his shoulders, and it made a deep impression on him.

I used to think how terrible always to be against your own people, always having to tell them what they don't want to hear. And then I began to understand what he must have felt. On the one hand I knew that I was free, but at the same time it became very hard. I knew I'd have to say what the Lord prompted me to say, but in doing so I'd be in constant conflict with the establishment, with my own people. Conflict is not an easy thing to live with. I used to say 'Lord, why must it be me who tells them?'

It was the old problem: was it that people wanted to be ignorant, or were they really ignorant? If they were really ignorant, then he felt he had a duty to present them with reality as he saw it. Time and again he would attend a meeting determined not to speak, and then find himself unable to keep silent in the face of opinions he felt to be blatantly wrong.

The family, too, began to notice Nico withdrawing more into himself. His joy of life, so marked as a young man, so cherished by his friends, slowly ebbed away.

There were times, too, when he would be shadowed by a deep gloom. He would identify with Jeremiah when he said: 'You have called me into a job that is breaking me . . . I mourn the day of my birth.'

Ellen would feel so sorry for him. 'It was like a fire the Lord had put in him, and he had to speak. He couldn't get rid of it, but I used to tell him that things weren't that bad.

Isaiah had had to walk around naked for three years, and some of the prophets married harlots, so really we'd been let off pretty lightly!'

Ellen was a constant source of comfort to Nico, but it took its toll. His moods affected her deeply, especially when he became remote and unresponsive. Then she would fly over the road (she was always in a hurry!) to Jetti Degenaar and let it all pour out. Jetti would listen with that gentle inner stillness that is part of her great attraction, and Ellen would return to Nico, ready to fight beside him for another day.

*   *   *

Student response to Nico was mixed. Looking back now, he thinks only about ten per cent went along with him, and there was a continual faction of right-wing students breaking away and complaining to the authorities about Nico's lectures. They were not, as one of his former students lovingly explains, riveting in their rhetoric. Nico was not one of the most dynamic of lecturers, but for those who had ears to hear, they were an inspiration.

A favourite phrase of Nico's was that it was time 'for the whole Church to bring the whole Gospel to the whole world.' The concept of the Kingdom of God that he tried to impart was that Kingdom meant not just the spiritual realm, but everything in creation. The Gospel had to be brought to bear on the social, political and economic realities of the world as well.

Nico was not alone among the lecturers in much of his thinking, but he was the only one who applied his theology to the practical issues of the day. His lectures were earthed in the reality of the times. One of his students, Wilhem van Deventer, who was to follow in Nico's footsteps as pastor of the hospital in Venda, remembers clearly the challenge of Nico's teaching.

He would speak about the importance of the Church getting involved; that whatever the political or social problems were, however big, the Church should tackle them. He expressed himself very clearly on issues like apartheid and racism.

In those days – the 70s – that was very radical. Everyone knew that everything was going wrong in the political, economic and social spheres in South Africa. It was the time when black consciousness was coming into the fore and there was this feeling in the air, but everyone was too afraid to get practical, except Nico.

For the majority of students Nico's classes became too controversial. They couldn't take the challenge and they would complain to the authorities about him.

But for the few, his lectures were an inspiration, and were to be a profound influence on their future ministries. Many sought his advice in private – it being too dangerous for them to be seen to be sympathetic to him during the public lectures. And on one occasion, when Nico had taken a particularly painful series of bashings from the Curatorium, a spokesman for a group of students came to visit him in his study. He had with him a statement they had drawn up to reassure Nico that they understood what he was trying to say and do and they believed he was right.

'It was worded in such a wonderful way that I just wept. I was so glad that something had really come through to them.'

16

CROSSROADS FOR NICO

Perhaps the greatest impact Nico had on his students was when, at their request, he took them to the notorious squatter camp at Crossroads. Here the students saw for the first time in their lives what it meant to live in utter poverty and squalor. For most of them it was the first time they had ever set foot in a non-white area. It was certainly the first time they had seen fellow human beings, mothers and children, living like rats in a debris of cardboard and polythene and sand, with no proper sanitation or water, in fact with none of the basic dignities or comforts which in their own lives they took for granted as necessities.

Eighty of them travelled in a hired coach to the camp on the Cape Flats. On the way they were singing and joking and making the usual student quips. They returned, four hours later, in virtual silence.

It was 1981 and Crossroads had been a running sore in South Africa for years as blacks from the homelands flooded into the Cape looking for work.

Legally, the only blacks allowed to live in townships in the 'white areas' were those who had been born there, or who qualified through long residence or employment, or who came on short-term contracts as migrant labourers from the homelands. But it didn't work out like that. Despite all the controls thousands of men and women would pour in from the homelands in search of work, especially during periods of economic expansion. They didn't have much choice in the matter, since there was no work for them at home. But by coming into the white areas without the correct stamp in their pass-books, they be-

came 'illegal', and could be arrested, imprisoned, fined and
deported.

David Harrison writes:

No one knows how many 'illegals' are in the cities; in
Soweto alone they may be half a million. What is known
is that they are the workers who will take any job that is
offered for pay well below the recognised rate, just to
keep body and soul together, and to send a postal order
to the family in the homelands, to buy school-books
and clothes and a better chance for the children ...
Employers like them because they make no demands
and do what they are told for fear of dismissal.

By 1974 there were thought to be about 90,000 'illegals' in
the Western Cape. There had been an economic boom in
the 1970s and thousands of blacks had come in from the
homelands to find work. When the boom ended, the
'illegals' stayed on, but because not a single house for
blacks had been built between 1972 and 1980, the squatter
problem became worse than ever.

Crossroads sprang up on waste land near Nyanga
township over the Easter weekend of 1975 and grew
steadily. Ten years later the official figures put the population at seventy thousand, but unofficially the numbers
were said to be far higher.

It embarrassed the government no end because it
pointed up the inefficiency of their influx control policy
and so in 1978, goaded by the extreme right wing of the
party, the government declared that Crossroads would
have to go. The bulldozers were put to work and the
demolition raids began.

BBC reporter Graham Leach:

The camp dwellers were living in rudimentary shacks of
cardboard boxes and plastic sheeting, their only protection against the bitter winds which sweep across the
Cape Flats in winter and against the scorching summer
sun. They became expert at burying the component
parts of their shacks in the sand each morning before

the demolition squads arrived, only to dig them out and re-erect them at night.

Many people were arrested, one died, as the bulldozers sought to flatten their makeshift homes, but the government was not able to break the spirit of the people, and as international outrage over the situation grew, so, too, did the Crossroads community.

In the winter of 1981, when Nico took the students, the homes of 150 families had been flattened by bulldozers and the people told they must go back to the Transkei. They refused. Instead the wives took their children and staged a protest outside the administrative buildings in Cape Town. They sat in the street, in the bitter cold and rain, with their children, for seventeen days.

Their conditions were so awful that the local churches rallied round and provided food and blankets and medicine. The only church that did nothing was the Dutch Reformed Church, and the students wanted to know why.

For several hours they talked to officials at the administration building and to the mothers and children. Then they visited Crossroads itself before taking the coach back to Stellenbosch, greatly subdued by all they had seen and heard.

It was a Friday and Nico told them to go home and think about what they had learned. They would talk it through at their lecture on Tuesday and draft a public statement when they had consolidated their views.

Nico recalls:

The students were very excited. They were pleased to be doing something practical in a situation like that. But somehow the newspapers got hold of it and phoned me asking if I'd made a statement, and if they could talk to the students themselves. I begged them to wait until Tuesday when we would discuss it properly together, and then we'd make our statement available to the press.

At midnight on Monday Nico received a phone call from the Dean of the Faculty. The scribe of the Curatorium had just phoned him. Some of the students who had visited Crossroads had been members of the Ruiterwag, the junior Broederbond, and had leaked to the Curatorium Nico's intention to draw up a public statement. Would Nico please call at the Dean's office at eight o'clock the following morning before he attended his lecture? Once again the Brotherhood had done its work and was moving frantically, and as so often, in the dark hours.

The scribe of the Curatorium took the lead. He'd asked the Dean to summon Nico because the Curatorium could not allow Nico to discuss matters like Crossroads with the students. Nor was he allowed to take the students outside the campus. Nor was it permissible for Nico to make a public statement with the students over what were essentially political issues.

It was a long hard discussion. Nico felt that as professional ethics demanded he be loyal to the Dean, he had to agree.

'I won't discuss it in class,' he said, 'and we won't draw up a statement, but I cannot allow you to limit my own conscience. I am going to make a personal statement on what I've seen and heard, but I will give it to the church press, and not the secular press. The church press can do with it what they will.'

When Nico told the class that he had been forbidden to discuss the Crossroads issue with them, there was nearly a riot. Those students who had been in sympathy with the issue were up in arms against their fellows for betraying them. But they would not be stopped altogether, they came to Nico secretly in ones and twos and in private conversations he continued to encourage them and to stimulate their consciences and their thinking.

He himself drew up a powerful statement in which he severely criticised the government and charged the Dutch Reformed Church with responsibility to act on behalf of the homeless. If the Church did not cry out against such an outrage as Crossroads, then it was an indication that the Church didn't care.

'Migrant labour,' he wrote, 'is inhuman and the Church must emphasise that it is a cancer in our society.'

The mud, once again, hit the fan. The church press printed it on their front page. The national newspapers took up the story, and started phoning Nico from all over the country. It became a very public issue and once again Nico received the inevitable summons to answer for his actions before the Curatorium.

But what Nico knew, and the Curatorium at that time did not, was that a far bigger storm was brewing; he and two friends had edited a book that was going to blow the lid right off the Broederbond and the DRC and Nico knew that once the Curatorium read that, his recent statements would pale into insignificance.

The book was to be called – aptly as it turned out – *Storm-Kompass* (*Storm-Compass*), and in it were essays by twenty-four of Afrikanerdom's leading intellectuals and theologians, including Johan Heyns, who attacked the DRC's support of apartheid, calling it to repent and to accelerate desegregation within the Church itself. DRC clergy and laymen were condemned for their unChristian attitudes and the unhealthy relationship between the Broederbond and the Church was revealed to the public in unequivocal detail.

As Nico stood in front of the curatorium answering for his public statement on the Crossroads incident he couldn't help thinking: 'Just wait till they read *Storm-Kompass!*'

None of them had to wait too long.

17

THE EYE OF THE STORM

Sunday Express, December 6th, 1981:

THE BOOK THAT BIT THE BROEDERBOND
Authors attack NGK's apartheid 'betrayal'

A book that could have a profound effect on the Afrikaans churches – and the country – was released in the Transvaal this week and is becoming an instant bestseller.

In a dramatic call to accelerate desegregation, the authors urge a complete U-turn by the White Afrikaans churches . . . they have shocked Afrikaans traditionalists by proposing some daring revisions of Afrikaner theology.

. . . a devastating frontal attack on traditional DRC theology . . .

The *Sunday Express*, in a full-page article, was just one of the many national papers that gave extensive coverage to the publication of *Storm-Kompass*.

The *Rand Daily Mail* reported exclusively on the revelations about the relationship between the Church and the Broederbond – still a daring topic to discuss publicly.

It had only been two years since Strydom and Wilkins' book had revealed the workings of the Bond and its membership for the very first time. They had made a list of all known Broederbond members – about 7,500 of them – which they thought represented sixty per cent of the full membership. Among these names were 750 Afrikaans clerics.

This revelation had been followed by immediate calls

from fellow churchmen and theologians to resign, the fear being that the clerics would be more loyal to the Broederbond than to the Church – a point of view substantiated in *Storm-Kompass*.

The man responsible for this chapter was Dr Jaques Kriel, Rector of the University of Bophuthatswana.

It was the 'practical experience' of many who attended church synods, he wrote, that Broederbonders conspired to influence decisions in a certain direction to such an extent that one delegate, in his frustration, once proposed that the synod's decision be prefaced with the words: 'We and the Broederbond have decided'.

The active interference by Broederbonders in synod decisions was not only documented, reported the *Rand Daily Mail*, but there was also proof that it was a deliberate part of the goals of the Broederbond to influence the Church in this way.

Dr Kriel asked if a church where at least sixty per cent of its clergy were members of a secret cultural-political organisation could still be called the Church of God? Could, and should, Christians, whose highest loyalty was to Christ and their fellow Christians, belong to a secret organisation? To Dr Kriel's mind they could not. And the church that allowed such a thing could not act as the body of Christ. The absolute integrity of the Church was put at risk.

Pointing out that on at least one point the Broederbond demanded a higher loyalty to itself than to Christ – a member had to lie about his membership and the activities of the Broederbond to fellow Christians – Dr Kriel wrote:

> From here it is just a small step to absolute loyalty to sectional interests and the specific ideologies of the organisation ... membership by Christians of secret organisations made it impossible for the Church to carry out its duty of reconciliation and bridge-building between people who would otherwise be worlds apart.

Professor Bernard Lategan, who was one of the three theologians who resigned from the Broederbond in 1979, also wrote in *Storm-Kompass*: 'In all openness and honesty we cannot bow our heads together before the same God in a situation of trust and searching for truth and the will of the Lord, if some of us are members of a secret organisation, even if the aims of the organisation are apparently also "Christian and holy".'

While publicity for the book came mainly from its attacks on the Broederbond, the *Express* pointed out the other controversies dealt with by the authors which they felt were 'far more explosive'. The book, they said:

Urges the DRC to confess to guilty complicity in injustices committed by Whites against Blacks and says it must now fight against apartheid.

Warns the Church that unless it eliminates racial barriers in its own structure it will become irrelevant in the 1980s.

Tells the DRC it should prepare Whites for a future as a minority in a South Africa where skin colour is no longer decisive.

The paper described the book as the most concentrated attack for twenty years on the DRC's alliance with Afrikaner nationalism and the government and its apartheid policy.

And they weren't exaggerating. The authors berated the Church for its indifference to racial injustices, accusing it of being a middle-class church interested only in defending the status quo and protecting the interest of the Afrikaners. They warned that if it didn't relax the colour bar within its own structures, the DRC would disappear as a religious force.

Summing up points raised in the twenty-four articles, Nico drew up an appendix of '44 Statements' – and it was this appendix, he thinks, which caused the most furore because it distilled so distinctly the views expressed that the implications were inescapable. For instance:

A Christian must never identify unreservedly with his *volk*, group, class or culture. His highest loyalty is exclusively to Jesus Christ as his Lord. Because the DRC has been so closely involved in the evolution of an Afrikaner identity, it has been guilty of placing Afrikaner unity above church unity.

True reconciliation could not take place in S.A. without a deep recognition and admission of guilt by all believers towards each other. The DRC ought to take the lead in this regard, confessing in humility and repentance the injustice which has been committed over a long period by whites against blacks.

The fact that some church councils still closed their church doors to believers of other colours pointed to a sinful refusal by Christians to accept each other as reconciled people.

Nothing could be more damaging to the credibility of the church in the world than the lack of love and unity which flows from it.

Loving your neighbour meant not only doing what you would have others do for you, but also not allowing anything to be done to another that you would not want done to yourself. In South Africa that meant, among other things, that the Christian could not be indifferent to the effects on blacks of the government policy of forced repatriation, or the sociological and emotional repercussions of migrant labour, or to the plight of millions of people who were crowded into black living areas, largely without basic amenities.

The Church in South Africa did not have the primary function of working for human rights, but of working for the human worth of all people. Human worth means that opportunity must be given to a person to fulfil his destiny as bearer of the image of God. Inhumanity involves all those factors, in and outside the individual, which hinder him fulfilling that destiny.

Storm-Kompass was described as 'a major offensive against the structural racism of the Afrikaans churches', and it left the establishment reeling.

Nico's old friend Carel Boshoff was chairman of the

Broederbond at the time. He dismissed the book's 'sweeping statements which would not stand the test of real investigation'.

For the next six weeks or more, letters of outrage and support – but mostly of outrage – poured out in the public press. The book was taken up abroad and some hope was expressed that at last the DRC was taking a serious look at the issues that had estranged it for so long from the rest of Christendom.

A side issue blew up because Professor Johan Heyns and Dr Pierre Rossouw, two contributors, said they were unhappy about the '44 Statements' and had not been told who the other contributors to the book would be. Letters in the press tried to make out that Nico had done the dirty on them, but he pointed out that the authors were responsible only for the articles under their own names, and that the statements were an accurate synopsis of the main points raised collectively by the authors.

That little row blew over and did not diminish the affection between Johan and Nico, though Nico believes Johan's concern was that the book as a whole made a more powerful statement than his old friend would have wished to make on his own.

Its publication was followed, of course, by the inevitable call to the Curatorium. Relationships between Nico and the university authorities were by now very strained indeed.

This time the Curatorium actually addressed the issue on hand. They said *Storm-Kompass* had been written by a handful of radicals known to Nico and that very few DRC ministers would share the same convictions. It was not in the least representative of the way people in the Church were thinking.

As they spoke, Nico's mind was on a tack of its own. If they thought *Storm-Kompass* was not representative, then he'd have to prove them wrong. He would write an open letter and send it round to as many ministers as he knew who might be sympathetic – at least two hundred he reckoned – and then send it to the moderature.

Strangely enough, although Nico was the one making

all the public statements, quite a number of his colleagues
in the faculty of theology had sympathy with his point of
view, and they were concerned that Nico was taking so
much stick from the Curatorium. Fifteen of them got
together and asked the Curatorium to explain why they
were being so tough on him.

They all met, Nico's fifteen colleagues, himself and all
the members of the Curatorium, to discuss the situation. It
was a wishy-washy affair. Vague statements were made
about the Curatorium not wishing to exercise undue restrictions on the professors, but nevertheless having to
play a difficult role in answering Church leaders about the
activities of the staff under their care.

The whole discussion was going nowhere until one
member of the executive asked if the meeting could become 'closed' – which meant that the deliberations would
be considered secret and all discussion outside the meeting forbidden. And it was agreed.

'Then I knew', Nico said. 'Now they could say what they
liked about me. They could attack me without reservation,
knowing that everyone in the room was bound to silence.
They said I was causing confusion among the students and
upsetting the Church. Church leaders wanted to know
why the Curatorium couldn't stop me and were pressurising the Faculty to shut me up. I seemed unrepentant
whenever they questioned me and my motives were
clearly political.

'What was so sad was that none of my colleagues stood
up for me. Not a word. They just let the others attack me. I
felt miserable. I was sitting there like a culprit and they
were all jumping up and down on me!

'Eventually I decided not to react. I felt I didn't have to.
They accused and I kept silent. I didn't speak.'

But that night, when he got back to Ellen, he was deeply
distressed. He knew the time had come when he had to
make a decision. Either he had to continue applying his
theology to the context in which he lived, speaking out as
he believed, and risk the inevitable sacking from his post,
or he must decide to keep quiet and have a restful life.

He didn't want to keep quiet, and he didn't want to be

sacked. If he was to leave Stellenbosch, he wanted to do it under his own steam. But no options occurred to him. The one thing he did know was that he couldn't go on much longer. He must make a decision. But to do what? The Lord would have to decide.

The next afternoon, at half-past three, there was a ring at the doorbell. Ellen was still at the hospital and Nico was alone in his study. He got up, opened the door and there was the postman with a telegram.

The postman stood on the doorstep as Nico opened it. It read: YOU ARE CALLED TO THE CONGREGATION OF MAMELODI, PRETORIA.

That's all. But it was enough. 'It was as if a voice from heaven had spoken to me. I immediately knew that I had to accept. I had prayed for guidance and the next day this extraordinary invitation had arrived. I had to believe it was from God. I read the telegram again and burst into tears! It was such an emotional moment. The poor postman just stood staring at me. He thought it was bad news.'

But when he went back to his study he began to have doubts about Ellen. Maybe she would think it absurd – to resign a professorship and go to a black township; to leave all they had built up in Stellenbosch and their lovely home. How could he ask her to give up everything they had?

When she came home, as usual, at five o'clock, they sat down for their ritual cup of coffee to exchange the news of the day. He let her start, and she told him what had happened at work, and who said what to whom.

Then it was his turn. He handed over the telegram and said, 'Look what came today.' Ellen read it over, paused, and then looking straight into Nico's eyes she said without a moment's hesitation, 'Of course, we'll have to go.'

On December 14th, 1981, five weeks after the publication of *Storm-Kompass*, Nico wrote a formal letter of resignation to the Rector of Stellenbosch University thanking him for the enriching time he had enjoyed at the university which, he believed, had prepared him for further service in the interest of the Gospel of Christ.

18

THE FINAL BOMBSHELL

'Normally the next step from being professor of theology at Stellenbosch is retirement and then heaven,' wrote one lady journalist. And certainly Nico's decision to go to Mamelodi was regarded as foolhardy, even by his closest friends.

Johannes Degenaar was among those who felt strongly that Nico was in a very strategic position at the university, able, as he was, to influence the thinking of the students. It would be wrong to throw this up for the obscurity of a black township.

I know there was some validity in these arguments, but I also knew that the circumstances under which the call came were too clearly an indication that God wanted me to go. I couldn't say no. And besides, I doubted if even 10 per cent of the students were sympathetic to my point of view, so my influence wasn't really very strong.

But it was painful. I remember many times I went into my study – I had a huge study lined with books – and I would say, 'But Lord, who's going to pack all these books?' And sometimes when I sat under the trees in the evening in our lovely garden I'd say, 'Lord, why don't you grant me the pleasure and the joy of just staying here?'

It was so painful to break away. We both wanted so much to stay in Stellenbosch.

For Ellen, who was brought up to relish lovely things, and for whom her home was a great source of delight, it was particularly difficult.

The church house was in Meyerspark, in the white suburb just outside the township, and I can remember so well the day we went to look at it. I cried all the way home! I couldn't bear to think that I was going to have to leave my home in Van der Stel Street for that.

That night I was still upset and it was as though the Lord himself spoke to me. His voice was so sad. He said: Foxes have their holes and the birds their nests, but the son of man had no place to rest his head. It was as if he was saying: that is what I did for you. I had nowhere to lay my head, but I promised to look after you, and you're going to have a house. I'm not asking you to live in a hole in the ground, or wander out into the velt.

'And I felt so ashamed,' says Ellen, her eyes full of self reproach.

But it was wonderful because it took away all my longing to stay in that Stellenbosch house. Now when I go back and see it I just think; well, what a lovely time we had there. It was a beautiful time in our lives, but I don't miss it, and I don't want to go back. The only thing I really lost was the nearness of Jetti. She was such a comfort to me, and the dearest of friends. There hasn't been anyone like her since then.

The only real fear about the move that Nico and Ellen had was that the call to Mamelodi might have been engineered by the Broederbond to get him out of the public eye, but a visit to Mamelodi soon reassured them and so in Nico's mind there really was no excuse for not taking up the post.

Other friends viewed his decision to go less charitably. Murray Jansön, who is also a psychologist, and whose love for Nico has a growing ambivalence, felt it was partly an expression of need on Nico's part to make his mark. As one of twelve siblings he would have had to fight very hard to get any form of recognition.

He is such a lovely fellow. He has empathy. He listens, but he loses perspective. He's never satisfied with ordinary things. He has to be right in the forefront. He's been an ordinary minister, and he did that very well.

Then he felt no, this is too ordinary, so he had the call to go into the mission field. So where did he go? Right out where there was nothing.

He was not the most exciting of lecturers and he knew the students were bored. He was at his wits' end. Fortunately for Nico, Crossroads came. It was the extra-theological things that saved him.

But this is all subconscious, and he's very humble. Nico would never think, 'I'm the boy,' but he has to excel.

Johan Heyns, on the other hand, feels that Nico's move to leave the Broederbond and to turn against the establishment was basically politically motivated, and that Nico then gave his political views a theological justification. Politics, in that sense, came first.

He thought Nico's acceptance of Mamelodi was 'not only unnecessary, but an outward token of his onesidedness, of leaving his own people'. And it's for this that Johan would most criticise his old friend. He says:

I can never ignore the fact that I'm an Afrikaner, and that I'm Afrikaans speaking, and if I really want to do something for other people, and that is naturally an obligation of being a Christian, then I can only do that if I, at the same time, accept myself for what I am. I cannot completely reject what I am. If I am going to do something for the blacks, I cannot do that by trying to be black myself. I would be completely untrue not only to myself, but to them.

I love Nico very, very much. Even though we disagree at times, we have never lost our love for one another. But I think, maybe, he tries to be someone he cannot be. I think that by his very strong identification and solidarity with the blacks he has lost his voice with the whites. Many whites do not trust him any more.

Heyns, on the other hand, is at present Moderator of the DRC, and a very influential man. He is still an active member of the Broederbond, and this aligns him so solidly with the establishment in the eyes of the blacks, that they don't trust him.

He would argue that the Broederbond is no longer concerned just with Afrikanerdom, and is doing 'a fine job' in terms of reconciliation. He also expresses a 'deep sympathy' with the black cause.

'But I've told him, Nico, if you really want to act as an agent of reconciliation you must bear in mind that there are two sides to the story. To put it very simply, there is a white side and a black side, those that are the guardians, and those whom we are looking after . . .'

Johan Heyns is physically one of those almost ugly men of great attraction. He has a strong but loving face which shows integrity and intelligence. He offers you plausible arguments in a book-lined study from a deep armchair.

But when you mull over what he has said, away from the seductive ambience of articulate and gentle reasonableness, you are left with the fear that this is a blinded man, keeping himself too safe, and that when the chariots of fire roll through the streets of South Africa, he will be one of those quickly consumed who leave no trace behind.

Whether Nico has gone overboard or not, you suspect that he and those he works with will leave behind them an inspiration of vision and courage – a rich inheritance for those who follow.

Nico explains his differences with Heyns by saying that Johan believes in identification, while he believes in confrontation.

'Unless you confront people with the realities and make them angry, they're not going to think about them. They're not going to get serious.'

Murray Jansön also believes in identification.

Murray is a very dear friend. I want to say that. But Murray is very dependent on the acceptance of others, that is why he could not make a clear break with the Broederbond, but just sort of slid out. He's a very popular man. The Afrikaner people love him. He preaches in a wonderful way. People cry when they hear him. It would be too hard for him to be rejected by these people. He would never be able to take it.

Sometimes I ask him; Murray, how on earth can you preach without making people furious? What do you say? Maybe he says it in such a way that people don't feel confronted.

But in his heart Nico thinks Murray has compromised; that his own world is too far away from the world of the poor and the oppressed for him to understand what it really means for the Gospel to be incarnate.

Murray, on the other hand, watches Nico from an increasing distance, clearly annoyed by some of his public utterances and by the growing international attention that surrounds him. Reading the foreign press, says Murray, you could be forgiven for thinking Nico Smith was the only Christian left in South Africa.

The general public also had their say about Nico's decision to leave Stellenbosch. He would pick up the phone to a string of abuse, always anonymous. He was a 'white pig'. He should go to the township so that 'when they shoot the kaffirs, they can shoot you as well'. He should be thrown to the sharks at Table Bay. Another well-wisher rang him up at 4am and deafened him with African music.

More articulate criticism came in the form of letters to the press. The *Sunday Times* reported on the 'Hate war on Professor'. He was dubbed a communist, accused of 'playing to the gallery', of irresponsibly disrupting the church, of drawing cheap attention to himself.

But Nico remained undaunted. He had one other little bombshell to drop before he finally waved goodbye to the ivory towers of Stellenbosch.

*   *   *

The idea that had germinated in his mind during his last session with the Curatorium had taken root. He decided to approach as many theologians and clerics in the DRC as he could, asking them to add their signatures to an open letter he had drafted calling for a change of social attitudes. He hoped that at least two hundred would sign.

That would certainly prove to the authorities that he was not a lone voice in the Church.

Nico knew that if the letter was to carry weight with the clergy, then it had to have the support of at least some of the country's leading theologians. To this end he first had his original draft vetted by three eminent Stellenbosch theologians, Professors Jaap Durandt, Bernard Lategan and Willie Jonker. All three approved the contents, but only one, Professor Durandt, said he was willing to sign.

The letter was then taken to another group of theologians in Pretoria who, to Nico's disappointment, reformulated some of the ideas. They placed the emphasis of the letter on the task of the Church in society, whereas Nico had wanted to stress the obligation of individual Christians to change their attitudes. Nevertheless, he agreed to the final drafting, and the letter was sent.

Basically it reiterated the main points of *Storm-Kompass* calling for a just society. The letter read:

> Justice, and not merely law and order, must be the guiding premise in ordering right society. We believe matters like the forced removal of people, the disruption of marriage and family bonds through migratory labour, under-expenditure on black education, insufficient and bad housing for black people, and low wages, cannot be reconciled with the demands in the Bible for justice and human dignity.

It argued that a dispensation in which irreconcilability was elevated to a principle of society and which alienated the various population groups, was unacceptable. That such a system made it virtually impossible for the people of South Africa really to know and trust each other and to be loyal to each other.

Laws which symbolised alienation between different people, like those on mixed marriages, race classification and group areas, could not be justified from Scripture, and while the importance of diversity was accepted, it was always secondary to the primary Scriptural principle of the unity of all Christians.

Of those who received the letter, 123 signed, and it was then published in *Die Kerkbode*, the official mouthpiece of the Church. Once again it was taken up by the national press. The *Rand Daily Mail* described it as 'an historical letter', a 'prophetic witness', and 'the most important development in the Afrikaans churches for more than twenty years.'

The letter of the 123 as it became known, caused an even bigger rumpus than *Storm-Kompass*. Published in June, it was still being debated in the national press the following September. It was held by many to be proof of the dangerous left-wing infiltration of the Church, worldwide. Dr H. B. Senelcal, from Bronkhorstspruit, called it, 'A calculated and structured leftist attack on the DRC to indoctrinate members.'

Some congregations lodged official complaints against their ministers if they had signed the letter. One church wanted the minister to resign, another called their pastor 'a priest of Baal'. Unsympathetic theologians said it had caused 'great unrest and confusion'.

The traditional Afrikaner view was typified by Dr Cruywagen of Kriel who wrote to the *Beeld* in September:

Many Christians in South Africa do not agree with the open letter. It is a plea for total equality, total swallowing up, total chaos and a total disappearance of Christian-democratic civilisation. In this reconciliation process the white church, national and Christian civilisation would be wiped out.

Referring to the breaking down of the colour bar within the Church as a whole, one 'Worried White' from Wellington wrote:

The coloured people have their own churches that were erected at great cost with the help of white congregations, and they are still being subsidised.
Why then, are the coloured people being forced upon us? We, the white DRC members, are entitled to our privacy. We shall be driven out of our own churches.

Regular attendance at meetings by coloured people is unacceptable. Leave the whites alone.

Perhaps the most common criticism levelled at Nico and his co-signatories, was that they were playing politics.

'Nothing can be more confusing and frustrating than the monotonous moaning about so-called discrimination and oppression by whites from theologians whose letters appear almost daily in the Afrikaans newspapers,' wrote a Tom Ferreira, of Graaff-Reinet. 'This attitude has made myself and many others, church-shy. These theologians must keep their noses out of politics and concentrate on their ministry.'

But as Nico told the *Weekend Argus*, it was not the intention of the letter to spell out any political policy for South Africa. Its intention was to make clear the Christian principles which should be functioning in society. Any political party which reflected these principles would obviously have the support of the 123. Any party which violated these principles would clearly see the open letter as a threat.

The open letter was to be Nico's swan-song as the 'turbulent priest' of Stellenbosch. Many of the friends and colleagues who so berated him during those days have now come round to a different point of view – though few seem to realise the scars their attitudes have left on the man they now profess to admire.

Charles Fensham is retired now. He hasn't officially resigned from the Broederbond, but he hardly ever attends the meetings. He's disillusioned and gentle. He concerns himself with ancient buildings and looks back on his life and friends with a loving eye.

One of the things I admire about Nico is his courage. And he's not just courageous in words, he's courageous in action. People used to say he wouldn't act the way he preached, but they were wrong. He moved to Mamelodi.

He's not a leader, you know. A leader is someone who takes the people with him, but Nico is way out in front. He's a prophet. He's not cautious, and when you move too far in front you're alone. Nobody is with you. Just a few might cheer you from the back, but they're not really with you.

Some say he was a traitor to the Afrikaner people, I don't believe that at all. But there is a price to pay for the sort of stance he has taken.

The price you pay is that friends leave you. Charles Fensham now has no recollection of cutting Nico off so brutally. Instead he gently suggests that the boot may be on the other foot.

'When friends criticise you, you begin to develop a fear that the friends have become associated with your enemies. You begin to evade them. You put the barriers up yourself.'

Be that as it may, it is interesting that of all the friends who now profess to admire and love Nico, not one has ever set foot in his house in Mamelodi.

19

FACE TO FACE WITH POLITICS

Father Trevor Huddleston wrote:

> It always amuses me to hear discussion on the hoary old
> problem of religion and politics and to think what such
> discussions would have meant to men like Jeremiah and
> Amos and Isaiah and Ezekiel. Half their time was spent
> in trying to bring home to the men of their day the fact
> that God was directly concerned in the way society was
> organised: in the way wealth was distributed; in the
> way men behaved to one another. In short – politics.

The reason why so many Christians were ready to excuse
themselves for 'conniving at injustice and oppression' was,
he felt, because of their totally wrong picture of Christ.

To so many the figure of Christ is the figure of the 'pale
Galilean' whose meekness and gentleness are utterly
incompatible with any concept of anger against social
evil or individual pride. To them all that is needed is 'the
art of being kind' and they think to see in Christ the
fullest and clearest expression of that art. Thus any
statement which seems to show signs of any intolerance
of such evils, or any passage in the Gospels which has
about it a denunciatory and threatening tone is hastily
forgotten.

But in fact there are many such passages, and to
ignore them is to mutilate the Gospel itself. Christ was
not afraid to tell his disciples that, in certain circumstances, they should turn their backs upon a village
which would not receive his teaching and shake the dust

from their feet as a sign that he had rejected that village utterly.

In his condemnation of the Pharisees for their distortion of the meaning of God's law and for their misleading emphasis upon legalism at the expense of life, there is no single note of gentleness, only a fierce anger.

In his teaching about the final judgment, Christ does not seek to soften in any way the punishments of those who have failed in their use of this life; indeed he reserves for them the most terrible words in the whole Gospel; 'Depart from me ye cursed into everlasting fire.'

And it is worth remembering that this condemnation is a judgment upon all who do not care for or concern themselves with the suffering of their fellow men. 'Inasmuch as ye did it not unto one of the least of these . . . ye did it not unto Me.'

The point I am trying to make is that Christian love is so searching, so demanding and so revolutionary in its force that it has no kind of relationship to the thing which is so often called by its name. No more than the Christ of the Gospels is like the shadowy sentimental figure so often invoked by Christians who want to live comfortably with injustice and intolerance.

One of the reasons why Christians are able to live so 'comfortably' with injustice and intolerance is that spiritual matters have been regarded by many churches over the centuries as 'other worldly' having little or nothing to do with the affairs of state or society. Spirituality has been seen as private and individualistic, and if anything is wrong with the world, then God is expected to intervene and put it right in his own good time.

This is the analysis of the Kairos Document, a significant commentary on the political situation and the role of the Church written by a group of South African theologians in 1985, of whom Nico himself was a signatory. They went on to argue that the Church had been unable to make any meaningful changes in society because it was politically uneducated and hadn't developed a social analysis that enabled it to understand the mechanics of injustice and oppression. It supported absolute principles like 'reconciliation' and 'non-violence' and 'peaceful solutions' and applied them indiscriminately and uncritically to every situation. They wrote:

> Changing the structures of a society is fundamentally a matter of politics. It requires a political strategy based upon a clear social or political analysis. The Church has to address itself to these strategies and to the analysis upon which they are based. It is into this political situation that the Church has to bring the Gospel. Not as an alternative solution to our problems as if the Gospel provided us with a non-political solution to political problems. There is no specifically Christian solution. There will be a Christian way of approaching the political solutions, a Christian spirit and motivation and attitude, but there is no way of bypassing politics and political strategies.

Yet this is a point of view to which, of all churches, the Dutch Reformed Church should be especially sympathetic. It's part of their Calvinist tradition to be involved in the things of the state. The outcry against Nico and those like him reveals an inherent dishonesty in the thinking of the Church in South Africa.

The Protestant Reformation had two main branches, the Lutheran and the Calvinist, which had two very different attitudes towards the state. The Lutheran's understanding was that you accepted the state. The Calvinist doctrine allowed that under provocation of a tyrant, you were called to oppose the state.

Where Calvinism spread, there tended to be intransigence and disruption – in Holland, France and in Scotland – whereas under the Lutheran German tradition, for example, the Christians far more readily signed allegiance to Hitler. Karl Barth, on the other hand, typified the Calvinist attitude.

The Dutch Reformed tradition is basically Calvinist. If they believe there is a tyranny above them, the clergy need have no hesitation in being involved in the call to arms. There is no stigma attached to a Calvinist minister involving himself with politics. That's why the Dutch Reformed ministers felt it permissible to join the Broeder-bond and the National Party in their struggle to free the Afrikaner people from British oppression.

The opposition to the mix of religion and politics comes from the pietist movement who are concerned only for man's soul, for man's salvation. They still feel that religion and politics should be kept strictly separate.

It's true that South African Calvinism has a pietistic element, but basically the Dutch Reformed Church is against Nico, not because he's mixing God and politics, but because he's on the wrong side. That is where the dishonesty lies. From the moment Nico began to apply his theology to the social issues of the day, and spoke out against the established church, he was 'accused' of being political. Worse, perhaps, he was accused of being naïvely political.

Johannes Degenaar, with whom Nico sat up on so many occasions to talk through his ideas, to clarify his thinking, knows Nico perhaps better than most and has his own view on religion and politics and on Nico's so-called naïvety. He says:

> It's a waste of time to talk about God if you do not respect me. I receive the quality of my life by the way you recognise me. If you say that Christ is incarnate in you, that Christ is incarnate in me, then the way we respond to each other is all important. And we must apply this criteria to the political situation in South Africa.
>
> Christ himself said that we cannot say we love God if we do not love our brother. The love he was talking about is not a wishy-washy love. It's a love that cares. It's a love that sees that the structures of society are worthwhile, are worthy of my brother, whom I love. So when people say that you can't mix politics with religion I would say that religion is politics, it's social concern.

His colleagues sometimes accuse Nico of being naïve. Maybe to begin with, he was. Maybe he still is. But if you've been brought up in an apartheid theology, and

God's world and this world are kept apart, and you're taught they can only be brought together via the church, and you discover that this isn't really happening, then your point is: How are we going to bring the Christian Gospel and relate it to the world in which we live?

Nico realised at a certain stage that he couldn't divorce his theological language from his everyday life, and then he started applying this in a more direct way. He started applying more consistently his religious commitments to the way in which the Dutch Reformed Church was structured. He was beginning to integrate his understanding of religion with his perception of the human state.

Maybe he hasn't yet worked right through to a political and economic understanding. There could be an element of truth in the criticism that he is naïve. If you are in a hurry to make a religious application of your faith in a political set-up and you don't understand the reality of economics and politics, there could be a problem.

For example, I think Nico, like Tutu and Boesak, would say that if we applied economic sanctions properly we would bring the government to its knees in three to six months. That is a nonsense. But there is a kind of religious fervour behind it. You want it to happen. But actually you have to acknowledge the power of governments and revolutionary groups and economic pressures.

The logic of politics is that you have to live with people you hate. You have to compromise, and on religious grounds it seems that is not the kind of language you would like to use. You would like to say it's all or nothing.

In Degenaar's mind it all comes down to the concept of politics being the 'interplay of pressures'. What he fears most – and what he suspects Nico might be guilty of – is 'redemptive politics'. Redemptive politics means that you are so certain that your own view is right, that you are concerned not with listening to others, but with converting them. If people do not agree with you, then they are not on the side of truth. The extreme of that position is when you say, 'I have to kill you because what you stand for is so evil that I cannot accept it any longer.'

Degenaar would not regard that as a political solution. He would call it the death of politics. If religion is about conversion, then it must be kept apart from politics, because politics is about compromise.

> By describing politics as an interplay of pressures you are safeguarding yourself from cherishing too high an expectation about what it can achieve.
>
> It protects us from the dramatic view of politics which is incapable of accommodating difference.
>
> It enables you to be critical of the misuse of politics by one group in dominating others. It creates space for free competition and for the co-operation between different groups in spite of their differences.
>
> And finally it guards you from harbouring the illusion that different political groups in a country can co-exist only on the condition that they share the same culture and agree on all issues.

So politics, as Degenaar sees it, is a question of compromise, not of conversion. It is a means by which a society can peaceably contain people of opposing views.

Degenaar thinks it could be argued that Nico was guilty of a redemptive approach to politics, of applying the old wrong-thinking to his new enlightened views.

> He seems sometimes to be saying that if we do not do 'x', then everything is lost. If you do not agree with him in what he's doing, then you're on the wrong side.
>
> I don't think this approach is helpful. It can play a role as one component in the South African context. It can be an irritant to make people think again.
>
> But Nico is doing a hell of a lot of other things as well. Just by going to live in Mamelodi he is giving a powerful testimony that there is transcendence in South Africa;

that there is religion and faith and hope in South Africa. His actions are a powerful symbol.

Maybe his just being there is more important than anything he actually says.

Degenaar thinks the cost for Nico of being politically naïve, perhaps, is that he falls into fits of pessimism because he's unrealistic about the political pressures. And there is something extreme in his nature – an all-or-nothing approach. There is a one-sidedness in his thinking.

Maybe his role in the body of Christ is to take the dramatic stand. But there is always a psychological cost to pay in an unbalanced life. You pay the price. You lose your relationships in the group you belonged to. But the point is that Nico is creating a new way of living. He's creating a new South Africa. And just living in Mamelodi is a symbol of that new South Africa.

20

THE CHALLENGE OF THE
INCARNATION

The name Mamelodi is taken from the Tswana, '*Tshwane ya Mamelodi*' meaning 'musical whistles from the Tswane River'. It's a pleasantly rural name for what must once have been a delightful piece of land, nestling, as it does, beneath the Magaliesberg mountains. The river is now hard to spot as it struggles through the uncut weeds and grasses, weaving its way round the piles of garbage that are the landmarks of the black township.

Officially there are only 106,740 residents in Mamelodi. The unofficial figure is nearer the three-hundred thousand mark. But there are fewer than 13,500 houses in the township – and most of these are little matchbox dwellings, known locally as 'four rooms'. In these four rooms, families of anything up to twenty-eight people may live.

Those who can't live in houses live in shacks made of hardboard and corrugated iron erected in other people's backyards. Shack-building is a full-time living for many. A shack-builder can charge between R150 and R200 for a one-roomed shack, and sell between fifteen and twenty a month. The housing shortage was so acute in 1984 that more than eighty shacks were being put up every month. They're illegal, of course, and the shack-dwellers live under constant threat of eviction.

Until 1980 all houses were rented from the government and no black person was allowed to carry out any repairs or improvements even if they had the money to do so. It was illegal even to paint the front door. The official reasoning behind this was to make living conditions so uncomfortable in the townships, so 'un-homely' that the blacks would not be tempted to stay, but would gravitate instead, back to their 'homelands'. By 1980 the government had realised that the urban blacks were a permanent fixture, and in order to encourage self-help in upgrading the townships, allowed the residents to carry out their own improvements and to buy and build their own homes.

The relaxing of the law produced a rash of exotic buildings. Today, interspersed among the 'four rooms', with their dirt yards and chicken-wire fences, are elaborate mansions, some with brick turrets like miniature castles, others with fancy stone-facings and stained-glass windows. There are double garages and profusions of draped net curtaining. These are the houses belonging to the middle-class and professional blacks.

More common are the modest improvements in the 'four rooms' of the poorer residents – a coloured window, a bright blue door, or a wrought-iron fence surrounding a still bare dirt yard.

Government money is now being spent in the townships, yet the amenities are still pitiable for so large a population. For the whole of Mamelodi there is only one day hospital with sixty beds. There are two post offices and two community centres, one cinema, one library and a police station. The untarred roads are full of potholes, the street lighting is spasmodic, the electricity supply erratic, often going off in the early evening and not being reconnected until the following day. Refuse collecting is irregular and inefficient.

Because there are no trees planted, no grass verges or proper pavements, the township in winter is a whirlwind of dust. It gets in your hair, it gets in your eyes, in your teeth and in your clothes. Together with the smoke that gathers from the hundreds of cooking fires and drifts through the open doors and windows, it makes life for the African woman very hard. It's a constant battle to keep your home and your family clean.

You boil your water in an old paint tin at the back, and with this you make your tea and wash your clothes and clean your body. Life becomes an endless round of cleaning and cooking and worrying because you haven't the money for soap, and you haven't the money for meat, and you haven't the money for school fees, and you haven't the money for clothes.

Yet despite the hardship of life in Mamelodi the township has always had a reputation for being politically quiet. And that's how Nico found it when he took up his new role as pastor in 1982.

He and Ellen had been given a manse to live in, about three kilometres outside the township in a fairly affluent white area. Ellen got a post at the black hospital of Medunsa 50 kilometres away, to which she travelled each day in her Mercedes-Benz – much to Nico's disgust! He bought a little truck and rattled around in that.

Ellen was unrepentant about the Mercedes. She'd spent too much of her married life bump starting Nico in old cars, and now was a time in their lives, she felt, when they needed something fast and reliable. If Nico was anxious that a Mercedes-Benz was not suitable for his image as a Christian, then maybe, his family suggested, he should learn to write travelling time into his diary, instead of arranging one meeting after another oblivious of the forty or so kilometres that separated them, and expecting Ellen to get him there on time.

Nico had been appointed as co-pastor to the church in Mamelodi. In the DRC tradition there is always a white pastor at a black church, and in Mamelodi, the black minister was the senior man. The principle was that they should liaise closely together sharing the work and vision for the church.

In reality, as Nico was to discover, his senior minister found it very difficult to work with a former professor. He felt threatened by Nico's presence, unable to meet him even for times of prayer.

Nico felt his first task should be to get to know the structures of his new church and to meet his parishioners. But his black colleague would not take him to the homes of the congregation. It wasn't as if he hadn't worked with a white before, but somehow Nico's very dedication threatened him. Previous white ministers had made very little contact with the people. Why should this new man be so keen to get involved?

In the end Nico visited on his own. During his first year he went out almost every evening, meeting as many parishioners as he could. Slowly he noticed their response to him changing. Most families had never had a white person call on them, let alone one who sat down and had a cup of tea, and really seemed interested in their lives. Gradually the old master-servant attitude was dropped. They began to relax and to open up as people, treating Nico not as 'baas', but as pastor and friend.

For him it was overwhelming – just the weight of their suffering. The most common problem was lack of money. They couldn't make their pay stretch far enough to pay for their children's education. Many young people were kept off school as a result.

Very often there would not be a single wage-earner in the house. 'How do you live?' Nico would ask. And they would tell of the auntie who had a pension and shared it with them, or a relative who was at work, or a grandparent who gave them food. Nico became very conscious that his own daily life centred around what he was going to do, while for most of his black congregation, life was centred around the problem of how they were going to survive.

At first he tried to solve all the problems. He wanted to act, to find solutions. Slowly he learnt that there were no solutions, and that just being with people, and listening and caring, meant more to them than anything else.

What the congregation of Mamelodi had expected from Nico when they called him is not clear. The church council had acted on the advice of one man, evangelist Eddie Manyakalla, who had first met Nico four years previously at a national conference. He had been deeply impressed by Nico's empathy with the blacks and the courage with which he had publicly denounced the racist attitudes of his Afrikaner background.

But no one else had really heard of Nico. He had been their second choice, the first man having declined. And

Nico himself was regarded as a non-starter because no one thought for a moment that a professor from Stellenbosch would give up his post to come to them.

'If he comes,' said Eddie to the church council, 'it will be because the Spirit of God has told him.'

But they had no knowledge of what he had been up to at Stellenbosch, or the public uproar he had been creating. All they knew was what Eddie had told them, that this white man had an extraordinary empathy with blacks. They had no idea that by accepting their call, Nico would be making history, or that Mamelodi would become the centre of a new movement of reconciliation.

While placing his work with the congregation as his first priority, Nico also took up two other important positions. He became a part-time lecturer at UNISA and, more significantly, chairman of the newly-resurrected Pretoria Council of Churches, known as the PCC. Although linked with the South African Council of Churches the Pretoria branch had quietly faded away through lack of vision. With Dr Nico Smith in the vicinity, new life seemed possible.

He was asked to help in re-establishing the PCC whose broad aims were to unite local churches in their action, both in society as a whole, and especially within the black townships. There was a seen need for real Christian unity, and for united social action.

Under Nico the council became actively involved in the needs of the people. He was especially concerned with those who were imprisoned, many without trial. In Mamelodi alone two hundred had been detained under the emergency regulations. Many were fathers and mothers, breadwinners. Who was to take care of their families? Who was to bring pressure to bear on the authorities to bring them to court? Who was to help arrange for legal representation? These were jobs Nico assigned to the PCC.

He developed a strategy of field-workers who visited the homes of people in distress to find out what their needs were, and how the churches could help. Sometimes these homes had been the target for township violence, bomb-ings and arson. Sometimes a young person had disappeared without trace, or a member of the family had been seriously injured. Wherever there was a need, someone would try to visit.

Although most of the mainline churches are connected with the PCC, very few have any personal connection with the work. They will send a representative to council meetings, but only one per cent of the money needed is donated locally, the rest comes from overseas. But this involvement at grass-roots level gave Nico added insight into the feelings of the people he wanted to serve. Watching him from a distance, the young people began to notice the depth of his commitment.

At this time two important organisations had already been set up in Mamelodi, the Detainees Support Committee and the Mamelodi Youth Organisation, known as MAYO, which was to become a major force in the community over the next two years. Even though some of its methods were aggressive, it had an impressive programme of alternative education and community responsibility.

The young people of Mamelodi saw themselves in the 'congress tradition', supporters of Mandela and Tambo, believing in 'non-racial' solutions as opposed to the more militant forms of black consciousness. As they watched Nico at work many felt drawn towards him. They began to ask him questions:

'Why do white people hate us? Why do they call us trash? Why must we always call them boss? Why must we accept it? Why do they give us a second-class education? Why do they want to keep us ignorant?'

Nico sensed that something was on the move. Something was brewing in the minds of these 'de-colonised' young people. They were the first generation of blacks to be born in an all-black community. Their parents had been born and brought up before the Group Areas Act had come into being. They had played with white and coloured kids in the street. They had absorbed the values of the colonisers. They had been brought up to believe without question that white meant 'boss', that without the white man they would have no jobs. That they were dependent on the whites. They had colonised minds.

But these young people that Nico was beginning to rub shoulders with had no personal experience of whites at all. No good experiences, anyway. They had never had white friends. Whites were the people who lived on the other side of the hill and who called them trash. They were the oppressors who stopped them experiencing real life in their own country.

Nico also became aware of an attitude of mind in the young which frightened him. They appeared to him at that time to have no hope for the future, to see their own futures as meaningless, and this, he sensed, gave them an insensitivity to life. They no longer cared if they lived or died, and they lost their scruples about killing others.

Paradoxically this seemed to be happening at a time when they were trying to take the future into their own hands, but it gave them a ruthlessness and reckless determination which they would not otherwise have had.

All these feelings they began to talk over with Nico, and their trust in him was to be a calming factor in the upsurge of violence that swept through Mamelodi and the other townships of South Africa in 1985.

*   *   *

Nico and Ellen had only been working in Mamelodi for about ten months when they went on a lecture tour of America. While they were there they heard an American called Henri Nouwen talking about incarnational theology – if you wanted really to minister to the poor, then you had to live as they lived. You had to be one of them, to experience the same problems, to live the same life, to share the same distresses. Only that way could you truly identify with those you had come to serve.

Nico and Ellen were both stunned as they heard Nouwen talk. In fact they were both in tears. Nothing had been further from their minds than that they should actually live among the 'four rooms' in Mamelodi. Now they knew they must, that nothing else made sense.

Nico found a book by John Perkins, the black American

pastor brought up in the deep South who had been beaten almost to death in the police cells during the 1970s for his work in the civil rights movement. It was called *With Justice for All*, and Nico went through it with a pencil marking up all the passages that reinforced what Henri Nouwen had been saying.

> If we are going to be the Body of Christ, shouldn't we do as he did? He didn't commute daily from heaven to earth to minister to us. Nor did he set up a mission compound which would make him immune to our problems. No, he became flesh and lived among us.
>
> God didn't have to become a man to find out what our needs were; but we needed him to become man so that we would know he knew our needs. Because he became one of us, we could be sure he understood.
>
> An outsider can seldom know the needs of the community well enough to know how best to respond to them. Without relocation, without living among the people, without actually becoming one of the people, it is impossible accurately to identify the needs as the people perceive them. Our best attempts to reach people from the outside will patronise them . . .
>
> Jesus was equal to God, yet he gave that up and took the form of a servant. He took on the likeness of man. He came and lived among us. He was called Immanuel, 'God with us'. The incarnation is the ultimate relocation.

Perkins went on to say that not only is the incarnation relocation, relocation is also incarnation. 'Not only did God relocate among us by taking the form of a man, but when a fellowship of believers relocates into a community, Christ incarnate invades that community. Christ, as his body, as his Church, comes to dwell there.'

But living among the poor in such a way, he argues, flies in the face of materialism. To consider it forces Christians to confront their own values. Have they accepted the world's values of upward mobility? Or have they accepted

God's values as demonstrated in the life of Jesus Christ?

This was the challenge to Nico and Ellen. They knew as they listened that day to Nouwen, that they were not doing what they should, that there was a further step they still had to take. But how, when the laws of the land forbade whites to live with blacks?

Nico and Ellen felt they had two options. They could either just find a little house in Mamelodi and move in, regardless of the law, and see what happened. Or they could make an official application to the Minister of Native Affairs requesting permission. In the end they decided to ask for official permission, and having written a personal letter stating his reasons, Nico waited for the outcome.

Within a few days he had an official acknowledgment that his request would receive attention. And then nothing. The weeks went by. Six months. Still no response from the authorities. And then one morning, nine months after his letter, Nico received a reply from the minister apologising for the delay, but saying the matter had had to be discussed by a number of people. They had decided to give the Smiths permission to live in Mamelodi, provided the city council also agreed.

The city council did agree, and the only problem that remained for Ellen and Nico was where to live and how. In the end they decided to build a small house, but it was to be round, modernising the concept of the African hut. It would prove cheaper than a conventional house, was different enough to be interesting, but small enough, they hoped, to be modest.

There was one central room downstairs with an open-plan kitchen, leading off it, a sliver of a bedroom, a shower-room and wc. The ceilings were made of pale wood, and so was the open staircase that wound up to the upper storey, which consisted of one large circular bedroom, a small spare room, and a beautiful tiled bathroom in pink and beige with all mod cons.

The local community were very puzzled by the whole edifice and would come and gaze at the builders as they pieced together the polygone roof. Some thought it must be a factory. Few thought it could be a home, but when the building was finally completed, and the number 7000 attached to the wall in big brass figures, half the children of Mamelodi, and not a few of their parents, trooped round it to have a look.

Just why the authorities finally gave them permission, Nico is unsure. As far as he knows he is the first Afrikaner ever to live in a black township.

'Maybe they thought I was so mad,' he says jokingly, 'that I might as well go and discover my madness!'

As it happened, when the time came for them to move in the authorities weren't the only ones who thought the Smiths mad. The trouble Nico had sensed brewing two years previously had flared into some of the worst violence seen in South African townships for some years. The spring of 1985 was not a sensible time for anyone, let alone a couple of honkies, to move into Mamelodi.

21
MAMELODI 1985

The papers were full of it.

June 8th, 1985
PUPILS HURT IN ALLEGED POLICE ACTION
A youth was shot and three others arrested after police dispersed a crowd of 1,000 chanting people marching from the funeral of a Mamelodi pupil at the weekend.

June 25th, 1985
POLICE SJAMBOK TOWNSHIP YOUTHS

July 16th, 1985
MAMELODI PUPILS DISRUPT CLASS
Pupils ... smashed several windows and forced children out of the classroom. This was the second incident of disturbances to occur at Mamelodi High School this week ...

July 18th, 1985
MAMELODI – PUPILS GO ON RAMPAGE
The car of a Mamelodi inspector was set alight and three buses stoned when boycotting local high-school pupils went on the rampage.

July 20th, 1985
PRESSURE BUILDS UP TO PUT STOP
TO VIOLENCE
Near anarchy flared in streets around South Africa again yesterday as pressure mounted on the government to put a stop to the violence.

July 21st, 1985
A STATE OF EMERGENCY IS CALLED
Press coverage to be carefully monitored.

July 23rd, 1985
WORLD REACTS WITH CALL FOR
MEANINGFUL REFORM

August 1st, 1985
FAMILY'S DESPERATE SEARCH FOR SON

A Mamelodi family has launched a search for their 13-
year-old son who disappeared more than two weeks ago . . .

August 12th, 1985
MAMELODI ERUPTS

Mamelodi is tense today after a weekend of violence that
saw two die, buildings in flames and repeated stonings.

August 16th, 1985
YOUTHS DEMANDED FUEL

A Mamelodi housewife told of her harrowing experience
when a band of youths demanded 10 litres of petrol from the
family car. The youths refused offers of money and forced
her to syphon petrol from the car. They told her to have the
tank full the following day as they would be back for more.
They did not return, but threatened to burn down her house
if she reported the matter to the police.

August 22nd, 1985: London
SOUTH AFRICAN TELEVISION IS KEEPING
WHITES IN THE DARK ABOUT THE
UNREST IN THE COUNTRY

August 25th, 1985
LAYABOUTS SHOULD BE IN WORK CAMPS

Unrest in black townships should be combated by clearing
out the 'layabouts' and putting them into work colonies, the
leader of the Herstigte National Party, Mr Jap Marais, said
on Saturday.

September 5th, 1985
TREURNICHT SAYS POLICE SHOULD
USE MORE FORCE

Dr Andries Treurnicht called on the government to 'un-
leash' the security forces to bring township unrest to an
end, instead of allowing them to use only bird-shot and
rubber bullets.

September 19th, 1985

Mamelodi town councillor's home was stoned and petrol
bombed for the second time in four days. All windows
smashed and furniture burned.

September 20th, 1985
BURNT MAN FOUND ALIVE IN HOSPITAL

A 23-year-old man who was kidnapped and set alight in
Mamelodi East after his home was attacked by a mob of
more than 300 youths, has been traced . . .

It was a frightening time for everyone in Mamelodi. The
various youth organisations which had formed themselves into the Youth Congress – youth meaning anyone
from 13 to 23 – had divided the township into areas which
were controlled by youth committees. The thinking behind their actions was to make the township ungovern-
able by the authorities so that the community could take
over its own affairs.

The problem, as the young people perceived it, was that
their parents were of the generation who believed there
was no way you could beat the system. They seemed
resigned to bowing their heads and getting on with life as
best they could, distancing themselves wherever possible
from unpleasant events.

The youth believed their primary role was to 'politicise'
the community so that it would respond as a united whole.
Polite requests to support the school boycotts, or the
consumer boycotts, or to attend the funerals of young
people killed in street clashes with police, were ignored,
and so the Youth Congress felt it had no alternative but to
try a more aggressive approach.

They intimidated systematically sections of the community at a time. In the evenings they would turn out the
lights and march through the streets, sometimes three
hundred of them at a time. Local residents were frightened and disorientated in the dark, not knowing what was
going to happen. They would hear bricks being thrown
through windows, the sounds of arguments and fighting.
They never knew whether the next knock would be at

their door. Many would just go to bed and stay there until the next morning.

Twelve days before Christmas 1985 the Youth Congress organised one of its consumer boycotts. They watched the white shops in Pretoria to take note of any blacks who entered and waited for returning residents at the bus-stops in Mamelodi. If any had broken the boycott, their shopping-bags were torn from them and the contents destroyed. There were numerous stories of shoppers being forced to drink their cooking oil and eat raw chicken as a punishment for breaking the boycotts. As a deterrent it worked.

The regulations under the state of emergency stipulated that only fifty people could attend a funeral at any one time, but whenever a young person was to be buried, a team of youths would knock on every door in the neighbourhood and tell residents to attend. If they refused the young people would threaten to burn their homes. No one in the house was excused, not old women, nor nursing mothers, even though mass attendance was likely to result in violent clashes with the police.

To consolidate their control of the community, the Youth Congress placed all sorts of social restrictions on the township and those that contravened these home-made laws had to appear before a 'People's Court'.

There was a time, for example, when parties were forbidden as a mark of respect for those who had died in the struggle. If a family wanted to celebrate a wedding, or a graduation, they had to apply for special permission from the Youth Congress. Anyone holding even a family gathering without special permission was liable to a visitation by several youths with sjamboks, who would threaten violence unless the guests dispersed.

Many residents lost money and even their jobs when work boycotts were called, but the young people seemed to discount the suffering they were causing their own community by depriving already poor families of any source of income. Now that it's all over, the older generation will shake their heads in wonder and tell you that, however extraordinary it seems, the fact remains that within a

relatively short space of time the young people of
Mamelodi were controlling the lives of the entire
township.

The Youth Congress still justifies this period of aggression. A young representative of MAYO explained:

Before the violence the people of Mamelodi were very
ignorant and unconcerned about what was going on.
The youth had to take extreme action because the
community would not listen. They had to be forced to
attend funerals because otherwise they stayed away
and distanced themselves from what was happening.
They had to be made to feel a sense of belonging. But it
was a pity it had to be done that way.

The problem with this method of 'ungovernability', as the
youth of other townships also discovered, was that they
could not control the natural thugs in their society who
used it as a cloak for their own criminal behaviour. Many
atrocities took place in the name of the struggle which had
nothing to do with the serious-minded young people who
were trying to bring the community into some form of
self-determination and control.

There was also little doubt by those involved that the
state began to employ black vigilantes at that time to
attack the houses of activists. It was then able to feed its
propaganda machine with stories of 'black on black' violence which in fact the state had instigated. In the end no
one was able to say for sure just who was behind the most
excessive violence. What is certain is that while the Youth
Congress were not averse to aggression, they were against
violence for its own sake.

While helping to organise the school boycotts, which
were the main thrust of the rebellion, the Youth Congress
had an impressive programme of alternative education.

One of their objections to black education – apart from
the fact that the syllabus was so limited that it did not
equip blacks to compete with whites when they reached
university level – was that it was so dull. Poorly-qualified
teachers taught in the 'teacher talk' tradition. They did all

the talking and the pupils were then sent away to reproduce what had been said. There was no pupil participation, no class discussion. There was no equipment in school laboratory work, no demonstrations in class. 'You learn to be certificated,' said one girl, 'not to know things.'

The Youth Congress ran Saturday schools. They realised pupils needed to get their certificates, but they also wanted them to be enriched.

We offered biology, English, geography, and so on, but approached the subjects in a more creative way. We linked them with reality. We introduced them to further learning – like astronomy. We'd make contacts overseas and people would send us teaching materials and equipment which in South Africa are normally only available to whites.

MAYO ran the schools and all the lessons were taken by the youth leaders themselves who were mainly university students.

They also ran a 'clean up' campaign. They would patrol the streets at night against crime. They collected sacks full of knives and offensive weapons which they had taken off local thugs, and they tackled the gangs who threatened and robbed local shop keepers. Because of their vigilance the incidence of rape fell quite dramatically. Even the police admitted to Nico that during the time the young had control over the township the crime rate was greatly reduced.

They also took steps literally to clean up Mamelodi. As far as the activists were concerned, the blacks on the town council were government stooges. The refuse collection was so inefficient under the local council, and the township in such a mess, that the young people refused to allow the town council trucks to remove the garbage. Instead they got hold of lorries and cleared the refuse themselves. For the first time the township began to look clean.

They started making proper pavements and to plant

trees and flowers. They made parks in the open spaces, the remains of which can still be seen. They often built 'cannons' from bits of old cars as symbols of the struggle.

During all this time Nico was in close contact with the young people. They had grown to trust him.

'When there were riots, when life was at stake, he was there. He is suffering with the people. He has identified with the people. They love him,' said a MAYO leader.

Many times this trust and love defused a volatile situation. The most testing time for Nico was the day when a young man was being buried. These funerals were always very tense, especially when the person had been killed during confrontations with the police. Hundreds of people would gather, singing their freedom songs, the atmosphere highly charged with every possibility of it getting quite out of hand.

Nico was not only afraid for himself, usually the only white man there, but also afraid that the soldiers would come and turn on the crowds.

One day, as he was leaving such a funeral, a young man came running up to Nico and pointed to a group that had gathered in a circle a little way off.

'You must come quickly,' he said, 'they're going to necklace an informer.'

There had been very few incidents of necklacing in Mamelodi and Nico was deeply shocked.

'At first I thought: I'm not going over. I'm going straight back to my car and drive home. I don't want anything to do with it. But then I thought I couldn't do that. This youngster was pleading with me to stop them.'

Nico's mind was a complete blank as he walked towards the ominous little circle. He didn't know what he should do or what he could say. And he was really afraid. Perhaps they would throw the petrol at him as well. With no words in his mouth and no confidence in his heart, Nico walked slowly into their midst. Into his mind came the old evangelical phrase: let go and let God.

A young man was being roughly held while a tyre was rammed down on to his shoulders.

I saw the look in their eyes. I was shocked to see such hatred. I just threw up my hands and said: In God's name, don't do this.

You have appointed your street committees. You have your People's Court. You have your leaders. Why do you want to pass judgment on this man now? Why don't you take him to your leaders and let them hear his case in the People's Court? If you take the law into your own hands now it will mean that your People's Courts are of no value, and your elected leaders are of no use.

It was suddenly very quiet. Nobody moved or said anything. Then, from one side, a group started to clap, and suddenly the whole atmosphere relaxed. The clapping was picked up by the crowd and they led the informer away.

'In situations like that you can't be brave,' says Nico. 'Maybe there are people who would not be afraid, but I felt real fear. It was the worst moment I ever experienced.'

Over the ensuing months Nico became very worried when he saw the way in which the young blacks were losing their sensitivity to life. Psychological studies elsewhere in the world had shown that people grew careless about their own lives when they found themselves trapped in situations which they could see no way of improving.

Nico felt this was happening to the young blacks in the townships. They did not mind committing suicide. They did not mind killing each other. They had lost their sensitivity to their own lives, and they had lost their sensitivity to others.

The necklacing incident was bad enough, but for the township as a whole, even worse was to come. In November 1985 an event took place which is now known to the locals as 'The Mamelodi Massacre'. It was the culmination of nearly a year of mounting tension and violence, and it was to lead to the final crushing of young people's control.

For some years there had been a growing dissatisfaction about rent increases. In 1983, under the new constitution, urban blacks were given their own local authorities which took on the responsibility of running the townships. But it

meant that they also had the responsibility of finding the
money to do it, and this resulted in massive rent increases.

Some residents received accounts with an almost thirty
per cent rise. The rise had come unannounced and
unexplained, and the residents were both confused and
angry about it. Many just couldn't pay.

Eventually, in November 1985, under the leadership of
the Youth Congress, residents held a meeting to discuss
the situation and it was decided that all the women of the
township should march to the new administration building and ask to see the mayor. Then they would put four
demands: that the rents be lowered; that restrictions on
funerals be lifted; that the police presence be removed
from the township; and that all the local councillors but
one (who had been selected by the people) resign.

On the evening of November 20th parties of young
people went round every house in Mamelodi knocking on
doors and telling the women in the families that they must
meet at the YMCA early the next morning to begin the
march. It had been decided that none of the young people
themselves would attend in the hope of avoiding trouble
with the police. Some of the women were to carry banners
which read: DON'T SHOOT OUR MOTHERS, THIS IS A
PEACEFUL MARCH.

People began to gather as early as 5am and by nine
o'clock in the morning a huge crowd had begun to walk to
the offices of the town council. Some reckon there were
thirty thousand, others put the figure at nearer fifty
thousand. No buses or taxis moved. The primary and
senior schools stood empty and thousands of commuters
were turned back by youths at the railway station. But the
swell of women and young children grew as they neared
the administration buildings.

So, too, did the presence of the police and army. A convoy
of riot police in eighteen armoured tanks and six police
vans gathered around the waiting crowd as they demanded to see the mayor. A contingent of *casspirs*,
Land-rovers and 'Mello yellow' vans also drew in close
until the whole crowd was encircled.

The women called for the mayor and he drove outside

the town hall in a military vehicle, which infuriated the crowd. He tried to speak to them through a megaphone, but they couldn't hear. The women started chanting: 'We can't hear you. We can't hear you.'

The police, fearing trouble, shouted at the crowd through their loudhailers: 'You have three minutes to disperse.' But the crowd was vast and hemmed in on all sides by military vehicles. It didn't know how to disperse.

Within three minutes a helicopter appeared and began to drop tear-gas canisters into the crowd. At the same time the police and army opened fire, using real bullets.

One eye-witness told the local paper:

The air was filled with the screams of women and children and gunshots. People seemed to be falling, overcome by the tear gas. Others were trampling the fallen. I ran, choking with the gas. I felt as if I was drowning. I thought I would collapse, but I kept running until I reached the clear air.

I saw people vomiting. A man lay in a pool of blood behind me. He was moaning, but I was afraid to look in his face. He was lying in an awkward position. I counted eight people lying motionless.

People were trying to revive an elderly woman lying face down. Someone turned her over. There was a huge wound in her chest.

Altogether thirteen women were shot in the massacre, and many more were injured.

The first official police report stated that they had opened fire 'after a mob attacked and stoned an SAP vehicle'. By the Sunday they had amended this to claim that they were forced to open fire when confronted by 'particularly vicious mobs' armed with petrol bombs and half bricks.

By the Monday an even more elaborate police report was issued alleging that they had given the crowd forty minutes to disperse because 'police feared for the marchers' own safety'. When this 'request' was ignored, the crowd was dispersed with tear-smoke. The crowd then attacked the police with petrol bombs, bricks and stones, and homes of police and councillors were set alight. Police had only used live ammunition in self-defence 'when their lives were endangered'.

Part of this statement is partially true. After the riot the young people did throw petrol bombs at the homes of black policemen and battles raged in the streets as youths set up barricades of burning tyres, old cars, rocks and municipal rubbish bins.

The sorrow of November 21st, 1985 is still vivid in the minds of Mamelodi residents. The women will stand at the street corner for hours telling you how they went with wet rags and Vaseline to rub round their eyes and noses as protection against the tear gas. All along they had feared the worst. They will tell you of the panic when the police turned on them, of not being able to see, of not knowing where to run, of stumbling over the bodies that fell. They try to explain what the tear gas feels like as it tears at your throat and eyes.

Two years later the people of Mamelodi were still withholding their rents in protest for the thirteen who died.

The march had taken place just before Nico and Ellen moved in, but news reached Nico almost as soon as it happened. He went over at once and found the township in a terrible state of confusion and anger.

A couple of nights later a delegation of young people came to him and said they wanted a public funeral for the victims and a big funeral meeting at the soccer stadium, but they were afraid the police would interfere and there would be another disaster. They asked Nico if he would contact the head of police and ask him to withdraw the military presence for that day.

Nico was not optimistic about his chances, but the next day he went to see the head of police who said he was willing to consider it provided a group of young people talked through the programme with some of his men.

There was no way the young would accede to that. They couldn't trust the police not to mark them out as leaders and arrest them, but they did agree to send some lawyers to negotiate on their behalf. The Police General agreed, and a meeting was arranged for the next day. It was to prove an eye-opener for Nico.

The following morning he went to the town hall with three black lawyers and a black businessman. The appointment was for ten o'clock. Ten o'clock came and went, but the police did not turn up.

Twenty minutes later they arrived, five of them: one general, the head of the security police, two brigadiers and two colonels. The two parties sat on opposite sides of a long table and the police took out their tape-recorder. To Nico's dismay, the chairman of his group immediately went into the attack.

'We all know that it's the soldiers and police who are responsible for all the unrest in the township . . .'

And Nico sat there in an agony of suspense and embarrassment as the chairman lashed into the armed forces with unremitting vigour. 'Dear Lord,' he breathed, 'now the ship is really sinking!' And he waited for the general to jump down the lawyer's throat. But he didn't. He remained perfectly calm.

'OK,' he said. 'Fine. Let's accept that we are responsible. Supposing we're not there, but the young people get out of hand and start throwing bombs and burning people. Who will control them?'

And slowly the conversation got under way. The lawyers couldn't guarantee the crowd's behaviour, of course, but felt it was important to show the young people that they trusted them. The two sides talked it over for an hour or more, and in such a good spirit, that when it was time to part each side thanked the other for being so reasonable. The police promised to keep away, and the lawyers for their part promised to call them in should trouble break out.

The next day the funeral took place. Nico was the only white person to be invited to speak. Thousands of people streamed into the stadium. They were singing and dancing, the young master of ceremonies handling the crowd like a professional.

The celebrations started at nine o'clock and they had promised the police to be finished by six that evening. For seven hours the people danced and sang their freedom songs and listened to the speeches of the chosen speakers.

At four the whole crowd went through to the cemetery, and just when the graves were being closed, Nico noticed a little knot of people gathering. Winnie Mandela had arrived, unannounced and unexpected.

Nico was horrified. She was still under detention and he feared the police would just move in and arrest her and mayhem would break loose. He told one of the organisers to tell the people they must return to the stadium immediately if they wanted to hear Mrs Mandela, and that she mustn't keep them longer than fifteen minutes. By this time the crowd was nearly ten thousand strong, but they fairly ran back along the road and Winnie Mandela inspired and encouraged them as they shouted and applauded her address.

By six o'clock that night there was not a single person left in the stadium.

The funeral was a major breakthrough for Nico. Everyone knew that he had been behind the negotiations and it cemented his relationships with the community in a way that perhaps nothing else could.

But Nico himself speaks with quiet respect for the senior police officer who refused to be baited, and who turned a potential confrontation into a moment of meeting.

22

BREAKING-POINT

Dr Smith is the white swallow
and he has come to live with the black swallows
beneath the Magaliesberg hills.
He has built himself a swallow's nest
among the four-rooms.
He has come to be among us
and to help us to fly free.

> Piet Mabuza – old evangelist
> Mamelodi, May 1987

To say it looks like a tip would be unfair. Everything in it
is too lovely for that. But certainly when you enter the
Smiths' little round house it does look a bit as if they're
getting ready for the movers.

The heavy front door opens straight into the front room
which is also the back room, the dining room and the
study. A lovely but large dining-room suite jostles for
space beside the comfortable armchairs. Flowering plants
straggle towards the light from big African pots on the
floor. There is just space for their two ancient King
Charles spaniels to wag their tails.

Elegant floor-length curtains are looped across the arch-
way that leads to the kitchen. The walls are lined with
books in English, Afrikaans, German and Dutch. Every
nook and cranny has an original lithograph or painting, a
gilt mirror, a memory of home.

The dining-table is permanently draped with a cloth of
hand-made lace, the silver cutlery lies on the kitchen
divide in open boxes lined with velvet. Everywhere you
look there's something lovely to see cluttered up beside the

paraphernalia of office life – the metal filing cabinet, the mini-switchboard by Nico's desk. Ellen's picture is in a little frame smiling behind the leather box of paper-clips and the plastic bottle of lemon water that Nico drinks continuously throughout the day.

There's nothing spartan about the way they live. There's wine in the fridge, olives in the cupboard. A large TV rests on a carved African chest beside a glass and pewter lampstand.

Not only must you pick your way through the furniture, across the little Persian rug and round the portable radiator, but you must also circumnavigate the bodies, because what little space is left in this living-cum-eating-cum-working room is usually filled with people. There are many local residents, often young, often in trouble, and there are frequently foreign journalists, visiting business-men, clergymen from overseas, students, diplomats, politicians.

It is not unusual to find Ellen sitting in a corner with a newspaper over her face, or resolutely watching the TV while Nico engages in an earnest conversation with three visitors just two feet away.

There is no privacy in this home. And despite all the lovely antiques and obvious signs of wealth, no pretence. It's the home of people who are living and who love – each other, other people, their family, the challenge of life. People not afraid to embrace pain, though they bleed, like everybody else.

For Ellen it is particularly hard. She gets up with Nico at four thirty every morning to read the Bible and pray. Then she drives an hour or so to the hospital where she is now professor of child psychiatry. After a long day with students and patients, there is the drive home. Katrinki, their maid, will have prepared the supper which she will eat, with a glass of wine, her eyes hardly remaining open. The front-door bell may ring three or four times during a meal, and the whole world pour in while Nico gets up to meet it. Nico never turns anyone away. There are times when, for the sake of their own personal sanity, Ellen would.

If she has one hour alone with Nico in the evening, she'll be lucky. Often she retires upstairs to their big upper room, with its dusty pink bed, and its plethora of family photos to have a quiet chat with one of her daughters on the phone, or to wash her hair, or to fall asleep while Nico goes on talking down below.

She goes with him to most of his evening meetings – at least they can be together in the car – and is accomplished at falling quietly asleep with a pleasant and intelligent look still on her face.

Despite the crippling pace of their lives, they are glad now that they live in Mamelodi, but the actual move was another matter.

For one thing, all their friends and most of their family were against it. The township was too dangerous. It was irresponsible of them to risk their lives. Johan Heyns was especially concerned and pleaded with Nico not to go. But Nico and Ellen felt that God had opened the door for them and they couldn't turn round now and say: Lord, we don't want to do it any more.

Only their children were philosophical. Maretha, their eldest daughter, is a sensitive and intelligent young woman who with her sisters has struggled to accept that her parents are dedicated to a cause that they put above family life.

'Once you've made your peace with that,' she says, looking at you with Nico's dark eyes, but with a perception that is very much her own, 'then you can accept what they do. By the time they wanted to move to Mamelodi I think the three of us felt that was the right thing to do. If we had put any emotional pressure on them to stop them going, they would have been unhappy. After all, it is their decision and God is with them. God protects them, and we can't stop them. What matters to me is that they're happy.'

When Maretha talks about her parents it's as if the roles are reversed. You have the strange sensation that she is the mother talking about two headstrong teenagers. And indeed, this is often how she feels.

I think all children who have parents who live a very idealistic and dedicated life have the same problem. You play the parent role. You are the one on whom they offload their burdens. But it doesn't work the other way around. You just have to accept that, that you'll never have parents in the conventional sense.

You may have parents up to a certain age who physically take care of you, but emotionally you're on your own. That can be difficult to handle.

And its hard having parents who are extra special. You always feel that you're being compared to them, and that you will always be less than them. Besides which you love them more than anyone else and you know them better than anyone else, and you also see a side of them that nobody else does!

When you're younger you long for an ordinary mother and father who will be there for you when you get home from school, on whose shoulder you can cry. But it doesn't work that way. When I was a teenager that was the hardest thing for me, to know that my parents weren't there for me.

Maretha and her two sisters were more aware than anyone else of the cost to Nico and Ellen of physically moving into Mamelodi. On the day the removers' van came, nothing was packed. They said it was because they had suddenly decided to move two weeks earlier than planned, but Maretha felt differently. She phoned that morning and found her parents deeply depressed.

'Although they were eager to go, they were reluctant as well. Although they were prepared to move physically, it was a great shock to them emotionally. The whole thing was more difficult for them than they realised. In the end the movers had to do the packing and I rushed over to them as soon as I had finished work.'

Nico remembers that day very well. He was terribly sad. He got a glimpse, he says, of what Abraham must have felt like having to leave his family and his country and go into an unknown situation. Because at that stage Mamelodi was unknown to them as a place to make their home.

How would the people react to them being there?
Wouldn't they just bomb their house right off? As one
friend had said, there was tremendous anti-white feeling.
They weren't going to preserve Nico Smith just because he
was Nico Smith.

And he and Ellen also realised that they had finally
made a break with their own culture, with their own
people. They were experiencing a major change in their
lives, moving out of the world in which they belonged.

Ellen felt it even more deeply than Nico. Her married
life had never been without its challenges, but this was
something different. Over the years she had moved from
the socially acceptable role of a minister's wife, with her
own medical practice, to the adventure of life in the bush
and the success of building a thriving mission hospital.
She had risen to the upper echelons of Afrikaner society in
Stellenbosch where she was known and loved for her own
achievements and had surrounded herself with all that
was gracious and lovely.

Now suddenly she was called to this – to live in the dust
and violence of a black township where the social roles
would be reversed. She would be the outsider, the despised
one, the hated white. She would live among the piles of
garbage and the backyard shacks, picking her way, in her
high-heeled shoes, across the potholes in the broken roads.

Quite a metamorphosis for the beautiful rich girl. But
then one thing in Ellen's adult life has never changed –
her obedience to the will of God as she perceived it. It is the
bedrock upon which she has built her life. And since her
marriage to Nico, she has placed her human loyalty
entirely with him. Where he felt he should go, Ellen
willingly follows.

Sometimes Ellen will come to you, when you are sitting
outside in a garden somewhere enjoying a meal, or a glass
of wine, and squat beside your chair.

'When I think of all we Afrikaners did to those dear
people,' she will say, her eyes filled with remorse, 'I
wonder if God will ever forgive us.'

Her commitment to a new society in South Africa is as
deep as Nico's. And she is willing to pay the price, the full

price, for what she believes. She is not afraid of death, only
of Nico's death. Her one prayer, in those early days, was
that if they came to shoot, they would come to shoot them
both.

Certainly the first night that they spent in their new
house in Mamelodi was a fearful one. Ellen, exhausted by
the traumas of the move, went fast asleep. But Nico lay
awake in dread. Would they come now? Would they come
this night? And what would they do when they came?

But no one came, and nothing happened. He was surprised by the cockerels at three in the morning. He had
expected to hear the birds at daybreak, but instead he
heard the dogs. There are few trees in Mamelodi.

In fact the local people were very positive towards them
from the first day. No whites had visited their manse in
Pretoria to see them off, but quite a crowd of blacks had
come to welcome them and offer their help – especially the
children.

The army instantly patrolled the road outside their
house. They were not rude, but they were not friendly. A
television crew had come to film their move, but they were
quickly sent away.

Every white visitor that came to see them from then on
was searched and questioned until Nico pointed out to the
authorities that since most of them were foreigners this
did not put South Africa in a very good light. The interference ceased.

Nevertheless these were tense times. There were
constant disruptions in the town. Houses were bombed,
people shot. Often it was impossible to tell who was
responsible for the shootings. Nico frequently suspected
the authorities.

There was provocation on both sides. The police had
begun to shoot at the young people with rubber bullets. A
new law was passed saying that anyone throwing a stone
at a military vehicle could be shot at random. The young,
seeing a 'hippo' pass by, would often make as if to pick up
stones, just to be provocative.

On one occasion a young boy did just that, and when the
soldier jumped out of the hippo to chase him away, the boy

ran. But the soldier was faster. The boy panicked and turned to face him, the stone in his hand, and the soldier shot him dead. The boy was 8 years old.

The township uprising was finally put down when the army was sent in. Army trucks accompanied town-council workers and stopped the young from refuse collecting and cleaning up the streets. They protected shoppers and commuters from harassment and rounded up the leaders of the Youth Congress. About two hundred young people were imprisoned and without them the boycotts and the programmes for alternative education and crime control came to an end.

To the relief of many residents, the period of 'ungovernability' was over.

A professor from Berlin who called to see Nico one day, told him of the research work he had been conducting into revolutions and riots all over the world since 1945. He discovered that ninety per cent of them were initiated by young people. His perception of South Africa was that the real liberation had already begun.

For those young leaders imprisoned, in Mamelodi and the other townships involved, there was a high price to pay. Official figures placed the number of young people detained without trial in 1984–6 as 11,000. The number held awaiting trial in police cells was officially as high as 173,000. Unofficially the figures are thought to be much higher.

And with arrest came torture. A report from one child welfare society in 1987 revealed that eighty per cent of children coming out of detention had been physically and emotionally abused, and most of the torture took place in the police cells. They suffered from beatings with sjamboks and rifle-butts. They were hit with fists and kicked, and some were beaten on the soles of their feet until they bled.

Sometimes the police tried to suffocate them, either with their bare hands, or by putting hoods over their heads which they tied tightly round their necks. One group of children reported being lined up naked against a wall while police threw stones at them. They scored one hundred points if they managed to hit the genitals or head.

Most of these young people had no recourse to legal help. They were detained without trial and released at the whim of the officials.

It was to Nico that families of those detained came in their distress. He would listen to their anxieties and wherever possible take up their case with the Pretoria Council of Churches, arranging for legal aid or pressurising for a trial. But in many cases he couldn't help. All he could do was listen.

What he and Ellen had not realised before they actually moved into Mamelodi, was that their house would become a refuge for those seeking advice and comfort. Knocks on the door would begin early in the morning and carry on way after dark. Nico was still a professor at UNISA with students to meet. He was chairman of the Pretoria Council of Churches. He was in constant demand from foreign and local journalists. He had mail from all over the world from people wishing to give aid, or be informed of the real situation. Because of the curb on the press Nico felt it extremely important that reliable information was disseminated to the press and foreign organisations about what was really going on.

He had also started an important new experiment in integration – Koinonia – which needed considerable time and effort, and on top of all this, he was still co-pastor of the local church.

Sometimes so many people came to see him that they would be waiting for their turn to speak, all cramped into the one living-room, with Nico trying to give each his undivided attention.

After eighteen months of this kind of pressure he became extremely depressed. The problems of the community were taking him over. He had no time to complete his other work. The pile of unmarked assignments, unanswered letters, grew on his desk. He felt he was drowning.

One of his problems was that he could never say no. Every letter, whoever it was from, he felt needed a full answer. No one was ever turned away. No invitation to speak was ever refused. He felt so passionately about what was happening that he didn't want to lose any opportunity to impart information. And he found it hard to delegate.

There was an even deeper price to pay – what his family perceived as a subtle change of character. Ellen described it as 'a quality of violence' that had entered his life. It was as if the violence he dealt with every day was rubbing off on him. He had become violent in the way he expressed his feelings, in the way he related to herself and the family. And it hurt her. It still hurts her.

> He was always a person with such a tenderness and mildness in his criticism of others, in his statements. He was always the one who cautioned the rest of us about being judgmental. Now that seems to have changed.
>
> I think he has tried to pacify the whites for so long that he can't do it any longer. He has tried for years to help them understand what was really going on, and he's lost patience. Now he says if they don't take a stand for righteousness, they're taking a stand against God. He's made his choice. He knows where he stands. He knows where he's going.

This very assertion that he's made his choice led his children to feel they could no longer talk to him. They feel he no longer listens to their point of view. That he's lost his objectivity.

Nico also perceived himself as being very much alone. Even those really close to him felt, and still feel, that he sees himself as far more alienated from people than he really is.

He would admit that the initial rejection from friends and colleagues has, generally, softened over the years, but says that their lives are now so different from his that they seem to inhabit different worlds. His brothers and sisters, scattered as they are all over the country, rarely meet with him. Some of his brothers still hold his political views with great mistrust, but they all profess to admire him.

'We didn't originally see that he was right,' says his sister, Barbara, 'but we've come to realise that he is. As time goes by we can see that his is the only way. But we're sad that there isn't more communication between us. We feel he has created a feeling of separation in his own heart. That he has put up the barriers.'

Whatever the true dynamics, Nico felt himself to be in continual battle with friends and colleagues. He felt compelled to be the one to make public utterance about his beliefs.

While there were growing numbers of young Afrikaners feeling the same way as Nico, and some formidable men before him – like Beyers Naudé – none of them had gone as far as living with the blacks and taking it upon themselves to share in the sufferings of the township as far as they were able. The strain on both Nico and Ellen, became unbearable.

Clearly something had to be done. Ellen put him on anti-depressants and had a pow-wow with the girls.

A young Baptist minister, Ivor Jenkins, had become involved in Koinonia, Nico's experiment in racial integration. He had already proved himself something of a rebel within the Baptist Church and was as dedicated as Nico to building a new society in South Africa. He was also a first-rate administrator, unflappable and fearless, and with the sense of humour and patience needed to cope with feet of clay.

Having persuaded Nico that he would not be able to continue without some sort of help, Ellen approached Ivor and asked him if he would become Nico's personal assistant. Ivor agreed.

For Nico, it was a turning-point. Ivor's salary was paid for by a group of Christians in the United States. A suitable house was found, a word processor and tape recorders installed. Slowly the mound of papers on Nico's desk shrank. His days became more ordered (travelling time was written into the daily diary). Bookshelves were put up and the last lingering cardboard boxes stacked away. More than that, he had an intelligent, sympathetic colleague with whom to share his feelings, if he so wished.

But it wasn't just Ivor that came to the rescue at this time. A friend found a little plot of virgin bush on high land about twenty-five kilometres from Mamelodi. He persuaded the Smiths to buy it, Nico and Ellen put up a small prefabricated house and two rondavels and to this little 'farm' they made their escape, each Friday night, for twenty-four hours of peace.

Gradually, glimpses of the old Nico returned. On a Saturday morning he could be found ambling between the bushes with a battered old hat and a packet of carrot seeds, or wandering around the emerging excavations for the farmhouse proper, gazing at the piles of bright red earth, and poring over the architect's drawings.

Ellen, still in her high heels, but wearing a shabby trouser-suit, would potter back and forth to the open fire putting vegetables and mealie meal into the big black cooking-pots, and cooing gently at her dogs.

The dusk falls slowly here, the sky changing from lemon yellow to a soft red as the sun gradually moves behind the hills. The only lights you can see are the lights of Mamelodi in the valley below.

This is the moment to see Nico Smith relaxed – sitting back in his deck-chair with the look of a man well pleased with his little piece of earth. The hoopoes grow noisy in the evening light and the prophet of doom sighs a gentle 'ya, ya, ya' and sniffs his Stellenbosch claret.

23

PEACE-LOVERS AND PEACEMAKERS

Leaving Stellenbosch for Mamelodi had been like returning once more to the real South Africa. For sixteen years
Nico lived in a beautiful environment with hardly a black
face in sight. The Cape coloureds had always been freer
and more Western in their outlook and the gulf between
the coloureds and the whites had not seemed nearly so
wide – at least from the white perspective.

Now he was back in Pretoria and the full ugliness of
apartheid hit him afresh. He was appalled by the psychological repercussions of the system. Shortly after the
National Party won the 1948 election, Nico remembers
hearing the Minister of Native Affairs speaking at a
public meeting.

'When you see black people in the streets,' he had said,
'remember from now on they do not belong here. They are
no longer part of our society. They belong to a homeland.
They are here only to perform a function, and when they
have performed that function they must return to their
homelands and build their own fatherland.'

Forty years later Nico could see that this attitude had
deeply affected the whites. There was now an alarmingly
impersonal relationship between black and white. The
enforced separation had lead to whites developing a
purely functional view of blacks. They had become imple-
ments for white use.

Because you did not see their husbands or wives, because their children no longer played with your children,
because they arrived from nowhere on your doorstep in the
morning and returned to nowhere at five o'clock, they had
ceased to be human. You didn't have to know where they

lived, if they were married, how their children were getting along. All that mattered was if they appeared and disappeared on time and performed their tasks adequately in between.

He saw that whites had developed an enormous fear of blacks. They were an unknown, impersonal force that threatened them – a fear subtly encouraged, he thought, by government-controlled newspapers which reported in detail crimes of violence by blacks against whites.

He noticed that the fences around white houses were getting higher and higher. Gates were now opened and closed with electronic devices. It would be nothing unusual to go into a house and see a shotgun in the hall, another in the dining-room and another, loaded and ready for use, in the sitting-room.

He didn't doubt for one moment that if the blacks ever rioted in the streets of Pretoria, the whites would not hesitate to shoot them down. It seemed to Nico that the most urgent task was to get black and white to meet each other again, at a meaningful level; to help them rediscover their mutual humanity.

In 1979 an evangelical organisation called Africa Enterprise had organised a huge meeting of South African Christian leaders (SACLA) of all ethnic backgrounds. About six thousand people had attended and it had been an emotional occasion with blacks and whites and coloureds reaffirming their commitment as Christians to one another. This had been followed by localised monthly meetings where small groups of Christians had gathered together in Pretoria to worship and call each other brother.

'Very pious,' says Nico, 'but it upset me. Here were the whites, thinking they had accepted the blacks, and asking them to come and meet them in their white town. And somehow they thought this was significant. When they asked me to come and address one of their meetings I felt I had to challenge them.'

In his much-dreaded role as Jeremiah, Nico punched it out. If they really wanted to do something significant, why didn't the whites complain to their MPs that their black

brothers and sisters had inferior education, that the
townships they lived in had no proper facilities? Why
didn't they make it clear that they as whites didn't want to
live in a society where they had more and better than their
fellow citizens?

And instead of meeting in a neutral white suburb, why
didn't they behave like real brothers and sisters and eat
together regularly in one another's homes?

The meeting listened to his views in a state of stunned
silence. As with most whites, especially Afrikaners, it was
the sharing of a meal which caused the biggest problem, so
deeply ingrained was this taboo. They also had a very real
fear of the townships. They had always been out of bounds
to the whites, and the recent outbursts of black violence
increased their anxiety. They asked for a month to think it
over.

Four weeks later they all met again. Significantly it was
the whites who brought up all the problems: how dangerous it would be to go into a black township; what about the
food, the blacks liked porridge and most whites couldn't
eat porridge and anyhow it would be so difficult to com-
municate with one another.

Having listened to all this for some time a black man
stood up and addressed the meeting:

I've listened to your problems. You talk about the dangers of the black townships, but not one of you has
expressed any concern for those of us who have to live
there all the time – and you call us your brothers and
sisters. Are you not concerned for our safety?

You worry about the food, but our women work in
white homes. We know what you like to eat. We've
been cooking for you for years. When you come to us for
a meal, we'll ask our wives to cook 'white food' for
you.

And what about communications? Are we not all
mothers and fathers, sisters and brothers? Do we not
have our humanity in common? And if you haven't
anything to tell us, we have a lot to tell you! You needn't
do the talking when you come, we'll do it.

In the end Nico took a vote. Who was willing to begin an experiment of reconciliation by sharing meals together in one another's homes? Seventeen people agreed, equally divided among blacks and whites, and so, amid much trepidation, Koinonia was born. Within three years it had spread nationwide and was to attract international attention. For many it became one of the rare flames of light in the gathering darkness of South Africa.

Koinonia means fellowship. It's a word used to express the spirit of generous sharing as opposed to the spirit of selfish getting. In the New Testament the word is used to express how wide and far-reaching this fellowship in the Christian life should be.

There is a 'koinonia' which means 'a sharing of friendship and an abiding in the company of others (Acts 2:42; 2 Cor. 6:14), and this friendship is based on common Christian knowledge. Only those who are friends with Christ can really be friends with each other. There is also a 'koinonia' which means 'practical sharing' with those less fortunate (Acts 2:44).

There is another use of the word koinonia meaning a partnership in the work of Christ (Phil. 1:5), a koinonia 'in the faith'. The clear implication is that the Christian is never an isolated unit, he is one of a believing company (Eph. 3:9).

There is also a fellowship, a koinonia 'in the spirit'. The Christian lives in the presence of the Holy Spirit, experiencing his company, his help and his guidance (2 Cor. 13:14; Phil. 2:1).

In the Christian life there is a koinonia 'with Christ'. Christians are called into fellowship with Christ. 'In the sacrament above all,' writes William Barclay, 'Christians find Christ and find each other. Further, that fellowship with Christ is fellowship with his sufferings.'

And finally there is koinonia with God (1 John 1:3).

In other words the Christian koinonia is that bond which binds Christians to each other, to Christ and to God. And this was the depth of commitment and identification that Nico was trying to engender in the Christians who expressed their desire to work for reconciliation and for peace.

But there is a world of difference between what he calls peace-lovers and peacemakers. It's one of his favourite themes. Most people, he believes, are peace-lovers. They want peace if possible, although it's actually hard for them to live in peace because it's contrary to human nature. Human beings are always in conflict one way or another.

But in South Africa, especially now that the tension is growing, most people want to find some sort of solution. Over the past three or four years the whites have suddenly discovered that they are alienated from the blacks, that they are strangers, that they have become their enemies. The youth uprising in Soweto in 1976 was quickly supressed, so it didn't really alarm them, but since the troubles of 1984 and the state of emergency, the whites have begun to realise that this problem isn't just going to go away and they want to find a way to 'normalise' relationships so that peace will be restored.

Over these years a galaxy of organisations has sprung up, all trying to work for better relations between black and white. At first the blacks were encouraging, but now they are getting gradually more disillusioned and Nico himself views them with open disdain.

Among the whites there is a deep feeling that they know best. Many people feel that if they can just get the blacks to understand that what the whites are doing is actually best for them, then the conflicts will be resolved. They seem to think that if they are willing just to meet the blacks, then the black people will say: well how kind of you to speak to us, now we really believe that you have good intentions and we accept what you're doing.

In November 1986 Nico was asked to address a group of representatives from different organisations in Pretoria who were working for better race relations. There were thirty-five people at the meeting, only three of whom were blacks. It was held on the eighth floor of one of the most

luxurious buildings in Pretoria with a panoramic view of
the white city. And here they were, meeting to discuss how
to co-operate with blacks for a better relationship. Nico
says:

> I felt so sad. First I told them that if they wanted to build
> new relationships, this wasn't the place to do it! We had
> to get out of the protected white world and meet in
> Mamelodi, or Atteridgeville.
>
> I told them I would be willing to set up a meeting in
> Mamelodi with the community leaders, especially the
> younger ones, so that they could find out from them
> what they felt were the causes of the unrest and tension.

The thirty-two whites tore into him. How could he consider anything as irresponsible as that? They all had
families to consider and God had given them minds to use
and going into Mamelodi at this time of unrest and hatred
against whites was clearly stupid. If they were to meet
with the black leaders at all it would have to be on neutral
ground. Not that they were particularly anxious to meet
the young black leaders. They were clearly all commun-
ists and there was no way they were going to allow them to
talk about restoring law and order.

'And that's the point,' says Nico, 'they were peace-lovers
but not peacemakers. Peacemaking is the willingness to
move into the conflict, into the area of tension. It is an
essential part of being a peacemaker that you make yourself vulnerable.'

He recalled the time when James Cone, the father of
black theology, came to UNISA to talk to the theologians.
The theologians got into a discussion that was way up in
the air. When they asked James Cone to comment, he said:

> I always thought that theology was everything to do
> with Jesus. I have listened to you for almost an hour
> discussing the Bible and God, but not once has anyone
> mentioned Jesus. What sort of theology are you actually
> practising?
>
> What I've heard this morning convinces me that in

South Africa you practise a Christianity that has Christ without his cross. If you take the cross from Christ, then he becomes irrelevant.

He went on to challenge them. If they really wanted to follow Christ then they had to go into the black townships and stand with the black people before the military vehicles, before the soldiers with their guns. It was in front of the soldiers that Jesus had taken up his cross. To be like Jesus you had to choose to become powerless and to experience what it meant to be powerless. It was in that situation that you would discover the cross of Christ.

Nico says:

To me, the main problem is that you have peace-loving people who are not willing to become involved, not willing to experience what it means to be powerless, to be unprotected, to be considered as a threat in your own country and to have no real privileges.

So many of them think that the only privilege you need as a black is to be able to live in your small house, and have your little job. You don't need more. What would you do with more? As a black you should think of all the other black African states and how terrible it is to live there with no jobs at all and even greater poverty. Here in South Africa you enjoy the privileges that the whites have created for you.

But a peacemaker, Nico believes, must have the willingness to allow somebody else to speak his mind. A peacemaker must be willing to listen and to argue, but not be threatened when ideas are put forward that are alien to his own. Above all he must be free from his preconceived ideas about black people. Most whites have been so indoctrinated that they believe every black leader is a communist, just because he's opposing the system.

He also believes that even people with very good intentions apostatise peace. They make it an absolute concept without considering what it is that causes the lack of peace. For him, as for other members of Koinonia, there can be no true reconciliation, no genuine peace, without justice. Any form of peace or reconciliation that allows oppression and injustice to continue is false.

It comes back to the misconception that if a Christian acts as a middleman, listening to both sides of the argument, and encourages the two sides to meet and negotiate, then he will be fulfilling his Christian duty by helping them to sort out their differences and the conflict will be resolved.

The Kairos theologians point out the fallacy of this argument. A private quarrel between two individuals or groups, whose differences are based on misunderstandings, can be resolved this way. But there are other conflicts where one side is right and the other wrong. There are conflicts that can only be described as the struggle between justice and injustice, good and evil, God and the devil.

> To speak of reconciling these two is not only a mistaken application of the Christian idea of reconciliation, it is a total betrayal of all that Christian faith has ever meant. Nowhere in the Bible or in Christian tradition has it ever been suggested that we ought to try to reconcile good and evil, God and the devil. We are supposed to do away with evil, injustice, oppression and sin – not come to terms with it. We are supposed to oppose, confront and reject the devil and not try to sup with the devil.

But the problem as Nico sees it is that many Christians in South Africa want cheap peace, a peace that can be obtained without a commitment to the cross of Christ. The peace they seek does not involve them in the conflict. It does not require them to take sides.

In a sermon on the prodigal son, the Rev. Dr Allan Boesak argued that too many Christians have been unwilling to understand that reconciliation was costly. He says:

> Forgiveness does not mean that sins are simply covered over, and reconciliation is never the pious concealment

of guilt. Reconciliation is exposure, the unmasking of sin, and a process of restitution.

Too long have Christians tried to achieve reconciliation by proclaiming a unity that rests on the cloaking of evil and a pious silence about the guilt they cannot face. Reconciliation is not holding hands and singing, 'black and white together – we shall overcome'. Reconciliation means sharing pain and suffering, accepting the other so that joy can be a joy together. It means the willingness to pay the price.

Reconciliation does not occur between the oppressor and the oppressed. Reconciliation occurs between people, people who face each other authentically, vulnerably, and yet with hope.

Nico is often criticised for being a 'prophet of doom' because he says that he can see no escape from the violence that is to come. That is because he doesn't believe it Scriptural to preserve peace 'at all costs' – especially at the cost of justice and truth. Rather he would argue with the Kairos theologians, that Christians should promote truth and justice at all costs – even at the cost of creating dissension and disunity and even conflict along the way. The true Christian approach is to engage in a direct confrontation with the forces of evil rather than to try and be reconciled with what is evil.

He would be more convinced by the white Christians who embraced their black brothers if they did so, not behind the plate-glass windows of a Pretoria skyscraper, but in the dusty streets before the soldiers and the armoured tanks.

*   *   *

Nico had even more challenges to throw down to that first little group of Koinonia members, but he felt that one hurdle at a time was enough! And for the whites, the first hurdle was to set foot inside the forbidden township and to eat the forbidden food.

The plan was that the couples should be divided into groups of four, and that once a month they should take it in turns to eat in one another's homes, alternating between the township and the white suburbs. At each meal every couple would bring a contribution. But the first meal was to take place in the township, after which they would all get together to find out how they'd got on.

When the debriefing took place Nico was thrilled to notice a marked difference in many of the whites. They seemed to be much freer in their relationships with the blacks. 'They didn't ask so many silly questions.' There was almost a feeling of celebration as they shared their experiences, a sense of liberation.

For blacks, as well as whites, that first meal had been a very emotional time. One lady said how frightened she had been just sitting in a white sitting-room because they had never been allowed to sit on a white person's chair before in case they made it dirty.

Another black lady who was a domestic servant well into her fifties, said it was the first time she had ever been invited into a white home, and it made her terribly nervous. 'We sat there in the sitting room and they were talking to me as a person,' she said. But it was when they went into the dining room to eat, that she experienced real joy.

'I thought this was heaven because I had always believed that one day in heaven we would all sit down together and celebrate. I felt the peace of God come down on us then.'

This joy was referred to time and time again by whites, too, who had taken a step 'outside the gate'. Many came to realise that they also had become victims of apartheid.

Willem de Villiers, brought up in the mainstream of Afrikanerdom, member of the Dutch Reformed Church, for ten years part of the South African Diplomatic Corps, would call himself a typical Afrikaner. He was brought up to think along racist lines, and when Ivor Jenkins first broached the idea of Koinonia, he was cagey.

He was suspicious that the Koinonia movement was 'way off to the left', that it was more political then religious, and it was only his friendship and trust in Ivor that persuaded him and his wife, Miriam, to give it a go.

But the memory of that first Koinonia meeting lives with
him still.

'It surprised me because it was so wonderful! I was
surprised by their very deep religious commitment, their
political awareness, the range and depth of our discussions. And I was sympathetic to their views. They
suffer. We were humbled by the depth of their Christian
insights.

'It was so strange that while we were living in cities
next door to each other, our views and experiences were
continents removed.'

That night, for Willem de Villiers, blacks became human beings for the first time. He felt, he said, liberated.

But not everybody could cope. One white doctor and his
wife withdrew because their neighbours were complaining about the blacks visiting them. They were afraid it
would harm his practice.

A black couple withdrew because their children had
said this was just another trick by the whites to soften
them up, and they shouldn't participate.

Others withdrew for no other reason than that they
couldn't take it. For those who stuck with it more
meaningful, cultural difficulties emerged. The whites, it
was generally agreed, talked too much. They were always
asking questions – which to the black mind is rude – and
getting impatient because nothing was being 'achieved'.

Francois du Toit, who later became organiser of Koinonia in Pretoria, felt a lot of the white responses were due to
a cultural aggressiveness and guilt. For one thing white
people felt that by talking they were communicating.
Nervousness and a fear of social silence led them to ask all
sorts of questions, and asking questions was a subconscious way of avoiding deeper communication which, especially for the Afrikaner, was very threatening. François
says:

One of the sacrifices of Koinonia is that you make
yourself vulnerable. You will find that blacks have
experienced a lot of hurts. If they get an opportunity to
open up and start sharing, they will tell you of all that

they have suffered, to such an extent that the white person begins to feel so guilty. They are filled with remorse. Some have said they felt they are being personally accused and that it was unjustified, because they were not personally guilty. But that is a price the whites have to pay. They have to be prepared to say they are sorry for what their brothers have done, sorry that they, too, are guilty, because they are part of the system.

Such openness takes courage, and not all the whites who joined Koinonia then, or later, were able to cope with it. Those that did were deeply moved by the healing that took place between them and their new black friends as a result. Together they discovered that to give and to accept forgiveness is one of the most wholesome experiences of the Christian life.

Another problem that emerged early on was that the whites were often frustrated that nothing seemed to be 'happening'. As they talked this over in their meetings it became clear that for the blacks, experiencing another person's company was an achievement in itself, meaningful and important. The whites, with their Western mentality, wanted to see something concrete emerge.

Francois had to explain that they were engaged in a slow process of healing. It wouldn't come overnight. It was more an evolution as two cultures learnt to merge into one community. They were learning to overcome the alienation that had developed between them, and to accept one another as fully human.

The blacks, too, had their problems. They had to unlearn the lessons of three hundred years. They had to understand that they were not inferior, that the whites were not gods. They, too, had to learn a new and more meaningful level of communication. And they had to forgive.

For both sides the physical dangers were real. Blacks were accused of being 'sell-outs' by their non-Christian neighbours. To be considered a sell-out could cost you your life. The whites, on the other hand, were the object of the hatred and violence, and there were times when it just wasn't safe for them to enter Mamelodi. On these occasions their black hosts would warn them on the phone, and the meeting would take place in the white suburbs instead.

Nevertheless, it soon became obvious that Koinonia, if it was to work, had to be more highly structured, and the goals expanded. There were tremendous logistical problems in getting the meal groups organised when one side had neither phones nor transport, and when the streets in the townships were unnamed.

It also became clear that the meal groups would need help if conversations and relationships were to become more meaningful. It was decided that the meeting should be structured. Since they had their Christianity in common, this was where conversations should begin. There should also be someone who led the evening, a convener, whose responsibility it was to lead the discussions and to be sensitive to the different needs in the groups.

It was agreed that each group of four couples should meet four times, and then split up and rejoin with a fresh set of couples. During the first meal they would each talk a little about themselves and their families. Then each couple would go home with work to prepare for the next meeting. That meeting would centre round what the Bible had to say about love and relationships. One couple would have swotted up on what Jesus said about love, another on what Paul said, another on what John said, and the fourth couple on what Peter said. All this they would share together.

By the third meeting most barriers were so well broken down that the groups abandoned their given subject and talked about the common things on their hearts: the situation in the country, education, the Christian witness and so on, but they could if they wished follow the set form of discussion laid down.

It was found that having a structure avoided initial embarrassments and helped couples get to know one another in a more natural way.

Slowly the idea of Koinonia spread. Other branches sprung up in towns all over South Africa. It was completely ecumenical, and by 1987 more than ten thousand Christians were involved. But it was clear to Nico and his team that just eating together was only the beginning.

Not entirely to their surprise the people of Mamelodi found themselves involved not only in feeding their new white friends, but in providing beds as well for all sorts of strangers whom Nico wanted to stay the night! It was time for whites to experience, at a deeper level, life in a black township.

24

LIFE ON THE OTHER SIDE

Looking through the fuzz of the net curtain I can see that the two houses on the opposite side of the road are tiny four rooms, still with their corrugated-iron roofs and faded blue front doors.

This house is large, crammed with heavy wooden furniture with red velveteen covers. There are nylon tiger-skin blankets on the bed and little crochet mats under everything. The bedroom is neatly cluttered with aerosols of hair spray and deodorant and bottles of red gel for black hair. A Mercedes-Benz takes up most of the driveway and there are mock marble surrounds round the wall sockets. In 1980 this was still a little four-roomed house, like everybody else's.

I am staying with Primrose's mother: everyone calls her Mama. Her husband was a taxi-driver with a fleet of cars, and she a matron in the hospital. Three years ago her husband dropped down dead with a coronary as he got up one morning to answer the front door. Mama found him lying on the floor in the sitting room. There are so few doctors in Mamelodi. She tried to resuscitate him for four hours before a doctor finally came.

In fact he had died immediately. 'But I dried up inside that day,' she says. 'I dried up from my umbilical right up to my throat. Only now am I beginning to cry.'

She still imagines him coming through the back door with his arms full of vegetables: tomatoes, onions, a chicken maybe. Sometimes she thinks she sees him in the street. He is always there, but never there.

Primrose's mother and her neighbour laugh as they sit round the dining-room table eating pap and gravy and describing the Mamelodi Massacre. Mama and her friends had run through the streets, eyes streaming, half blinded by the tear gas, terrified that one of the soldiers would get them. They ran along the alleyways to their homes, dodging in and out of the houses, hiding where they could when the army hippos passed. It was hours before they finally made it home, they say, popping in another mouthful of pap with delicate fingers and wiping the tears of mirth from their eyes.

Mama's neighbour has a large firm bosom with a brooch pinned on it which reads MOTHER, and it shakes up and down as she laughs.

How can they laugh when they talk about such things?

> Because my mouth is wide with laughter
> You do not hear my inner cry.
> Because my feet are gay with dancing
> You do not know I die.

I never knew who wrote that verse, and I never experienced, until now, the full pain of their meaning.

Mama was on the parents' committee that was formed to talk to the children about why they were rioting and boycotting schools. But she couldn't understand them. They spoke, she says, but they didn't tell.

They said they wanted better education and complained about school uniform, but it was much deeper than that. But the children couldn't, or wouldn't, articulate it.

The young blamed her generation for not fighting. 'Ever since Soweto,' she said, 'things have not been the same,' and she takes the chicken-neck from the stewpot and bites it off a piece at a time, sucking noisily between her teeth.

'You see,' she says, 'how I eat it?' and she takes a clean bone from her mouth. 'I eat it vertebra by vertebra.' Soon a little pile of bones lies beside her plate, and Mama sighs.

I was not the first white to sleep in peace in her big wooden double bed beneath the nylon tiger skins. Mama is part of Koinonia, just one of the many Mamelodi residents who open their homes and move out of their beds to give hospitality to visiting whites. Most of the homes are very humble, and most of the whites are very apprehensive.

That would certainly describe the state of mind of one Afrikaner clergyman, from the Western Cape, who was visiting Pretoria with a party of clergy to talk to church leaders – radicals and the non-radicals – about the current situation. At Nico's suggestion he agreed to spend his last night in the township, but not without some trepidation. He described his experience to the Koinonia team afterwards.

'When darkness fell on Mamelodi,' he recalls, 'and thousands of people were on the streets; when I heard the noise and thought about everything I'd ever read about the black townships, I have to admit that my heart was beating in my throat.'

This Afrikaner dominie was about to experience something that would have been quite unthinkable even a couple of years before, something that would have made his forebears turn in their graves. He was going not only to eat with a black family in their home, he was going to share their bathroom and sleep in their bed – and he was extremely nervous.

The house was terribly small and, when we were having supper, crammed. But the rooms were sparkling clean, far cleaner than ours at home.

When we eventually retired for the night – having talked the hindlegs off a donkey – my colleague and I realised to our dismay that our black host and his wife had given up their own room and their own beds for us. I still don't know where they slept that night.

But the one moment I shall never forget as long as I live was when, after our long discussions, we had family devotions together. Our host opened the Bible and read from it. His wife and children led the singing. We sang the Our Father in Afrikaans, like the church choir in the black congregations often do. And then we prayed. Each one had a turn.

It may sound strange, perhaps even funny, but I

felt almost as if I was back with my grandfather and grandmother round the supper table.

It was clearly a deeply moving experience.

Some English critics have suggested that this form of getting together is just 'tokenism', just a sophisticated form of social tourism – a criticism the Koinonia team strongly refute. They believe that there is a Biblical principle involved. Christians call themselves a community of believers, and this belief has to be made concrete reality. Living in community means, among other things, identifying with one another. In a society as alienated and polarised as South Africa, the intimacy of spending a night as part of the family is an important first step.

Identifying also means listening. The blacks often accuse the whites of not listening, and of thinking they can talk for everyone else. The missiologist Walter Trobisch once wrote that God had equipped us for life and our calling with two ears and one mouth – and that we should learn to use them in that order.

For the Afrikaners who realised for the first time what it meant to listen and to share at a meaningful level, the Koinonia experience has proved to be one of the most meaningful in their lives. It is not unusual to hear them speak of a new joy and freedom as a result of this, their first step, outside the gate.

It soon became clear to the Koinonia leaders that more than just shared hospitality was needed. They had to work together, and learn together, if they were to build their new relationships. Monthly meetings for all members were held at which visiting speakers opened up topics of national interest that affected interpersonal relationships in the country. They became important not only in terms of education, but in giving members a chance to talk over their views and problems, political, social and spiritual.

New projects emerged. A youth group was started. Cinemas had just become legally opened to all races, but very few blacks had had the courage to test it out. Koinonia youth groups went in parties of six or so to test the law, and to witness to their belief in a multiracial society.

One or two restaurants in Pretoria also opened their doors to blacks, and once again the youth tested them. Here they frequently met with abuse and insults from other customers who were offended at the presence of blacks. But the proprietors gave their tacit approval by not asking the young people to leave, but rather allowing the other customers to walk out.

These were not easy evenings to handle. Sometimes it was hard to say who was most upset by the insults, the blacks or their white friends. But it bound them closer together and was a public statement of their commitment to one another.

This commitment did not come naturally to many of them. For the blacks, who had no positive experience of whites, a great deal of suspicion had to be broken down. The young whites, on the other hand, had to learn that their attitudes were frequently condescending, that they too had been indoctrinated to think they were superior and this arrogance was often unconsciously present, even when they felt themselves to be free of it.

Young blacks suffered from a sense of deep frustration that their parents had allowed themselves to become demoralised by the system, had accepted the view that blacks were somehow inferior. Young whites, on the other hand, began to experience an anger against their own culture for the wrong values that had led to the present crisis and put them in such an invidious position. Many of them now had to face the possibility of army call-up for a cause they were vehemently against.

These emotions have not been easy for either side to handle and they will tell you that some of the most meaningful moments in Koinonia meetings have been when individuals have felt free enough to express their anger, or their pain or their humiliation, and have received love and support in return.

The young people also decided to turn their hand to a little work. A scheme was set up to start 'beautifying' Mamelodi – taking up where the Youth Congress had left

off. Having talked to the residents it seemed one of the
most urgent needs was to repair the roofs of the poorer
houses, and the people of Mamelodi, who once looked with
some amazement at the white pastor and his wife in their
midst, have now grown used to the sight of their own
young people running up and down ladders with their new
white friends.

At the moment the work goes on in holiday time, but the
young have a dream for the not too distant future – to set
up a commune in the township where they can live and
work together.

Nico believes passionately that caring means action,
and he is slowly moving the Koinonia groups into new
areas of social involvement. For some time now a Koinonia pre-school centre has been opened up next door to his
house, and more than sixty children go there every day. It
is run by two teachers and a cook, all full-time, and
employed by Koinonia. They have also opened up a small
curio shop where locals can sell their crafts.

But the depth of need in the community has persuaded him that what is really needed is a whole social
work complex. It will be the first of its kind in South
Africa.

The dream is to have facilities for social work and family
planning; an information centre where legal advice will be
available, and information on housing and employment.
There will be an education centre for multiracial educational projects and a finance bureau to assist with loans,
bursaries and relief funds.

The idea is that the centre would also incorporate the
Koinonia Commune and provide accommodation for overseas visitors to Mamelodi, as well as conference halls. The
curio shop would be expanded into a centre for handicrafts
and self-help employment. By early 1988 a few sponsors
had already come forward promising money, but a massive amount will be needed for this dream to be fulfilled.
Meanwhile Ivor and Nico plan on in faith.

Nearly all of Koinonia's projects have been funded by
people from outside South Africa and the extent of international concern for the project is reflected by the number

of foreign journalists and television crew who descend on Nico throughout the year.

In March 1988 Koinonia SA and the National Initiative for Reconciliation held a conference with a difference. Called 'Christian Encounter in Mamelodi', the idea was not to cram people into a crowded conference hall to hear speakers read intelligent papers on the subject of reconciliation. Rather the conference was to be an opportunity for delegates to experience another side of life.

Over 170 white and brown delegates were accommodated in black homes and about thirty-five blacks stayed in the white suburbs. The four-day conference was so structured that people had time for meaningful discussion and interaction; they shared meals and relaxation time together in private homes; they worshipped together and had a taste, albeit a small one, of what it was like to live in an environment so different from their own. This experience then became part of the input for the sessions of reflection and interaction led by guest speakers during the day.

Nico and Ivor knew that they would get good press coverage, but they were not expecting the fourteen international television crews that turned up to film the conference along with all the other newspaper and magazine journalists.

However encouraged they are by the interest the world at large is taking in the work of Koinonia, the fact remains that ten thousand people is a very small percentage of the population of South Africa. With more money, and a more sophisticated administration, Nico believes the Koinonia concept could grow, but even so, it will always remain a group on the fringes of society.

This doesn't discourage Nico or his colleagues. He says:

I've told the people, we're not trying to prevent a revolution, that isn't possible. It is going to happen whatever we do. But we must get together so that, together, we can go through the disaster.

I believe that if we can develop small groups of people in as many places as possible all over the country, after the revolution, these people will be able to pick up the pieces and build a new South Africa. It is only the Christians who have learnt to love one another now, who will be able to rise like a phoenix from the ashes.

Dr Klaus Nurnberger, one of South Africa's foremost theologians, expressed a similar view when he addressed one of Koinonia's monthly meetings.

He cited the small groups of German Christians who in the early 1930s foresaw that Germany was heading for a catastrophe. They began then to build up a new system of values and relationships, and when, in 1945, Germany was in ruins, its people demoralised, its industries and cities destroyed, these Christians played a vital contribution in the rebuilding of their country because they had already discovered an alternative way.

He said:

The lesson for us is clear. We must begin to look beyond the present crisis. South Africa will continue regardless. There is a future to be built. And the sooner we begin to build that future the better.

However small the group, there must be some who know where we are heading, who have begun accepting new values, who have begun to build new relationships, who have begun designing new institutional structures.

Let us bring our hope down to earth. Yes, our hope is in Christ. Our hope transcends all frustrations and catastrophes in this world. We shall be with God in heaven. Christ prepares for us a dwelling there. Being assured of heaven – do we not hope for the earth?

We cannot have hope in God and be hopeless for the world which God loves. Christians cannot afford to lose hope. Love cannot afford to lose hope. People with vision transcend everyday desires and enmities. There is a task ahead for us to accomplish. Let us go forward with joy and confidence.

But whatever hope of real reconciliation was alive in the hearts of the few – it was not reflected in the results of the May election of 1987. The Liberal Party, that so many thinking whites had pinned their hopes on, was badly defeated. The National Party won another clear victory, the only noticeable swing being not to the left, but to the right.

25

A NEW HEAVEN AND A NEW EARTH

The results of the 1987 general election on May 6th were crushing, not only to any hopes among the blacks that a more liberal government would be elected, but to the growing number of white South Africans who longed for change and saw only too clearly what an escalation of violence would mean. They knew how sophisticated and powerful the South African military really was.

One big Afrikaner sat at his desk and wept at the memory of what he had been made to do and see when he did his national call-up. He told his friend of the black wounded they were not allowed to tend, because their bodies were booby-trapped; of the black pregnant woman shot in the street, her guts and her unborn baby splattered at his feet. Even after ten years the memory haunted him and he cradled his head and cried at the thought of what would happen if a full-scale civil war ever erupted.

So deep was the mood of despair among enlightened Christians that all the bishops of the Province of Southern Africa met in La Verna a few days later and issued this public letter:

> We are conscious of much that is good in our land; of courage and love in spite of adverse conditions; of schools seeking to build bridges; and individuals and congregations who go to great lengths to break down the partitions which divide us. We are grateful to God and to them for that. Yet we also live at a time when many people have lost all hope of reaching a peaceful settlement in our land.
>
> The General Election has made it clear that most

white people prefer the so-called 'security' of guns to that created by faith in a loving God, and in love and sharing. Preoccupied with 'minority rights' white people cling to power in a way which denies the love and gentleness of our Lord who prayed for forgiveness for those who executed him.

We believe that the 'swing to the right' in white politics indicates to black people that they are not cared for, nor do the laws of the land protect them.

In a land where the State of Emergency allows the government to use indiscriminate violence to support its policies, where detention without trial is normal; where ideologies in the townships create their own internal violence, where fear, bitterness and resentment overwhelm us all; where raids and threats of raids into neighbouring states are becoming increasingly frequent; where the war in Namibia is regarded by many as a war of occupation by South Africa, and suspicion and mistrust are a way of life in most of Southern Africa;

We call on the people of God, in the power of the Spirit, and in the name of Jesus, to cast away their fear, suspicion and mistrust;

To look up and see each other as people beloved of God, for whom Christ died;

To pray for each other, even if we see the other as our enemy;

To build bridges of mutual caring, of giving and receiving of each other's divine gifts of love and humanity;

To worship together, to speak together, to pray together and to seek recreation together;

To start to build up the people of God so that God be seen to reign;

To give costly witness to the values of the Gospel in the struggle for God's justice in our land.

We are confident that the loving God whom we worship and serve is involved, caring, feeling and listens to prayer. We are confident that God in Christ overcomes evil, and good will therefore prevail. We are confident that when we care for the broken and the damaged, the poor and the oppressed, we are doing God's will, healing the hurts and revealing his kingdom.

We are confident that when we repent he freely forgives. We are confident in God, not in the vaunted security of any cult of wealth, or programme of change, any dispensation, ideology or system . . .

We are confident that the gates of hell shall never prevail against God's church, but through his son, God will build his kingdom and every power and authority will be trodden under his feet.

Be confident with us: Jesus is Lord. He is risen, Alleluia.

Few could echo that Alleluia except in the blind and obedient faith that Christians are called to exercise in the face of seeming hopelessness.

'To uphold faith and hope in these dark days of crisis is what it means to be the servants of God,' wrote Desmond Tutu.

If you ask Nico how he continues to have faith in God despite his apparent absence, he will tell you that his personal experience of God is so real, and so frequent, that he does not doubt either God's existence, or his love. To this knowledge he clings, even in the darkness.

And the darkness is real. Despite the promises of the Botha government, he sees no real reforms. It has become clear to the National Party that apartheid as originally conceived will not work. The urban blacks have to be integrated into society, and their life, therefore, made more tolerable so that they become more acquiescent and are built up into a quiet middle class whose vested interests, it is hoped, would inhibit them from encouraging a revolution.

But liberal whites are kidding themselves, says Nico, if they think real reform will ever come through the Botha régime. The only real change he can envisage is a move to the right.

He is not alone in thinking that no real reforms will ever take place under the present government. Sampie

Terreblanche, who has finally taken up the cudgels in Stellenbosch where Nico left off, has described the National Party as 'a captive of multiple captivities'.

Quite apart from anything else it has become a captive of its old age as a governing party. It's been in office for forty consecutive years, and during that time has never really been forced to re-examine its approach. Terreblanche would argue that it has lost the ability to appraise and identify the real causes of South Africa's problems. It has become the victim of all kinds of frozen perceptions.

The National Party has tried through its propaganda, to persuade the white electorate that it is the only party in a position to bring stability to the country and to avert a total disaster. The one party that can create new hope. To Terreblanche, nothing could be further from the truth. It is the one party incapable of meaningful change.

He is also deeply pessimistic about South Africa's future from a purely economic point of view. He believes the government's recalcitrant attitude and lack of sensitivity towards the demands of the Western world to end apartheid has resulted in an isolation and divestment that have had a devastating effect on the country's economy. In the last thirteen years South Africa has experienced a negative growth rate.

Since 1974 the average growth rate has been 1.8 per cent with a population growth rate of between 2.3 and 3.5 per cent. If this government stays in power we'll be lucky to maintain even a 1.8 growth rate.

From 1974 to the end of the century, the population will double from 25 million to 50 million, but during that whole period the growth rate will be negative. The poverty in the black townships and the shanty towns will be something terrible.

He points out that poverty is now beginning to creep into white circles. In the last six years the after-tax spending money of whites has declined by twenty per cent. Now they're living off their earnings.

A colleague calculated that if South Africa managed to reach a growth rate of three per cent from 1984 to the year 2000 they would still only be able to create enough job opportunities to accommodate the people who entered the job market in one of those sixteen years.

But the government refuse to listen to men like Sampie Terreblanche. They tell him that they are tired of his alarmist theories.

They have a naïve belief that next year we shall see a turn in the economy and then we'll have a growth rate of 5 per cent or more. They have no conception of how terrible the conditions are.

Economically we cannot go it alone. We must create signs of hope. The government must prove with visible evidence that it really intends to dismantle apartheid, then hopefully we can restore our relationships with the Western world, because sanctions have undermined confidence in the South African economy. We are slowly, but certainly, bleeding to death.

As the poor get poorer, he believes the motivation for revolution becomes stronger.

'Forty-five per cent of all whites in this country are now under 25, and they are rich and terribly spoiled. Almost sixty-five per cent of all the black children are under 25, and they are not only poor, but the majority of them are also embittered. How are we to bridge the gap between these spoiled children on the one hand and these embittered poor blacks?'

One of the ways, Nico believes, would be to release Nelson Mandela and the other political prisoners, un-ban the ANC and begin meaningful conversations with its leaders, but this the government refuses to do.

Botha forbade Nico to take a party of Dutch Reformed pastors to Lusaka to meet the senior men of the ANC. Nico himself has, since then, had several meetings with ANC leaders, not because he is party political, or trying to co-operate with them in the purely political sense, but because he believes no meaningful change is re-

motely possible unless the ANC – as the black people's
accepted leaders – are engaged in planning for a new
future.

White South Africans keep saying that we are making
reforms. Who are the 'we'? It's actually reform according
to the white standards, according to white understanding of reform. But it's not an honest, radical willingness
to start negotiating with the real black leaders to work
out a new political dispensation in which all the inhabi-
tants of the country will participate.

Botha is not willing to negotiate with the liberation
movements. He's not willing to liberate the political
prisoners. He's not willing to take away the Group
Areas Act or the Race Classification Act. In that sense,
despite all the so-called reforms, he is maintaining the
status quo.

There is a French proverb which says you make
changes in order that things can remain the same.

A new generation of intellectuals is now following in
Nico's footsteps – meeting with ANC leaders and trying to
address themselves to the problems of fundamental
change – but between them and Nico you sense a mutual
weariness.

Nico gets exasperated, not only by their belated understanding of the situation, but at their refusal to look at the
reality as he sees it – that civil war is unavoidable.

They, on the other hand, become clearly wearied by his
prophecies of doom. Many are still struggling to find a way
out of the situation which will not involve them in too
radical a change of life style or commitment. Their criticism of Nico is that he has moved out of the white arena
and nailed his colours firmly to the mast of black emanci-
pation. Now, they argue, he sees everything only from the
black point of view.

Nico is not apologetic. He has lost his patience with
those whites who can clearly identify oppression, but
refuse to endanger their own privileges by acting radi-
cally. People, like his dear friends Johan Heyns and

Murray Jansön, who are still, he feels, trying to please both sides.

Sampie Terreblanche believes now that Tutu was right when he said it was those who still insisted on remaining 'part of the clan', who were the real stumbling-block to reform.

During the time of the May elections, the World Council of Churches held a conference in Lusaka on 'The Church and the Search for Justice and Peace in South Africa'. Dr Klaus Nurnberger returned from that conference a disturbed man.

The realisation haunted me that the reconcilers and bridge-builders who try to step into the breach between the warring parties are being co-opted by, or forced into either of the camps. And the side where you are located physically in the social structure, will probably be the side which can exert greater pressure on you, in spite of all your commitment to social justice. I do not live in a township, but in a white suburb . . .

Right in the middle of the conference the white electorate solidified behind those who will not grant Namibia its independence, who promised not justice but state security, who will not negotiate a constitution based on equal rights with authentic black leaders, for whom 'power sharing' means nothing but co-option into a system determined by whites, who will keep the lid down on the boiling townships by force of arms, who will attack front-line states 'harbouring terrorists'.

The message that came from the election was that the white population was ready to fight. It had the character of a declaration of war . . . It became clear to us that the mere fact of [our] having spoken to the ANC could be construed by the majority of white South Africans as conspiracy and treason.

Where is the place of the peacemaker when the battle is in progress? Love and reason, their only weapons, seem to be no match for guns and propaganda. It takes faith not to despair.

Nico does not despair, but he does not harbour false
illusions. He sees no short-cut through the deepening
violence.

> I believe God is sending the whole nation through a
> process of catharsis. We have to go through it, we have
> to have the cross and the crucifixion before there is
> resurrection.
>
> The reason why people see me as a prophet of doom is
> because I want to put the whole truth on the table and
> say: let us face it. Don't hope and pray that this isn't
> going to happen. It is. Accept it and pray to God that we
> may get through it somehow and be purified by it.
>
> I believe the whites will have to suffer God's anger
> and judgment. If you really know what we've done, and
> if you look at it in its totality, then I can't see how God
> can just allow it to pass by silently.

It has been argued by those who closely identify with Nico
that his aggressiveness, his delight, almost, in forecasting
devastation for South Africa, is not the best way to win
converts to his point of view.

Ivor Jenkins feels that when Nico so vehemently
portrays a hopeless message, people stop listening to him.

> Many whites read him as saying that we need violence.
> I've heard him say that myself. But if somebody
> motivates me negatively, I just cut off.
>
> This is what's happening to Nico in some circles at the
> moment. His words are unacceptable to many whites
> and moderate blacks. Some people you need to offend,
> but on the whole you have to keep a balance between
> challenge and hope.

It's interesting that when projecting the future, Nico
always refers to South Africa 'after the revolution', and
Ivor refers to 'post-apartheid' South Africa.

But the tragedy that Nico foresees is that the longer the
present situation continues, the more damage will be done
to the country as a whole, especially in terms of human

relationships. He feels the young blacks are becoming more brutal and that they want violence because they've come to the conclusion that there is no other way of breaking down the present structures.

This violence he sees being reflected in the new black consciousness movement. All the more reason why the whites should respond now to the ANC, who still believe in their original freedom charter and in a non-racial society. Should the emerging black consciousness movement take over from the ANC, then all hopes of peaceful negotiations, he believes, would be lost.

He never forgets the remark of one black colleague who said; 'By the time the whites have decided to love the blacks, the blacks might have decided to hate the whites.' He says:

My hope and my courage are in the fact that I know there is a new future to come. The existing injustices will be broken down and at least there will be the possibility of saying let's try to create something new. Even if it may in the beginning be worse.

People accuse me of being naïve to trust in the humanity of the blacks. But I do trust their humanity.

I don't say it's going to be heaven when the blacks or the ANC take over. In some ways it's going to be hell. But why not? As long as justice is exercised.

And if you say to me that justice will not be exercised, then I say we must fight again for justice under the new régime. What we have now is evil. We must get rid of it. Whether it's going to be worse under a new régime is not my concern at the moment. You cannot condone one evil fearing that if you fight it another will take its place. But if it does, we'll fight again.

But why must we expect the new régime to be worse than the present? Why? Why can't we expect to be surprised by love?

Nico believes that God wants justice and peace in his creation, and that he has been called to be one of the many engaged in the struggle to bring that about. There are times along the road when he sees clearly the hand of God at work. There are times when all is darkness. But he never loses sight of the vision written down by St John in Revelation 21:1–5.

> Then I saw a new heaven and a new earth . . . I heard a loud voice speaking from the throne: 'Now God's home is with mankind. He will live with them . . . He will wipe away all tears from their eyes. There will be no more death, no more grief or crying or pain. The old things have disappeared . . . And now I make all things new!'

Nico Smith does not doubt that one day this vision will become reality for South Africa.

SELECT BIBLIOGRAPHY

Of the numerous sources used for the preparation of this book the following were invaluable and would provide the reader with stimulating background reading:

David Harrison *The White Tribe of Africa* (Ariel Books, BBC, London, 1981)

Graham Leach *South Africa* (Methuen, London, 1986)

I. Wilkins and H. Strydom *The Super-Afrikaners* (Jonathan Ball, Johannesburg, 1978)

Sipo E. Mzimela *Apartheid: South African Naziism* (Vantage Press, New York, 1983)

John Perkins *With Justice for All* (Regal Books, California, 1982)

Trevor Huddleston *Naught for your Comfort* (Fontana, London, 1956)

The Kairos Document – A theological comment on the political crisis in South Africa (Skotaville Publishers, Braamfontein, South Africa)

GLOSSARY

Apartheid – apartness, separation

Bantu – The People, used now as a singular noun to denote a black man

Baas – boss

Broederbond – Band of Brothers, Afrikaner secret society

Casspirs – armoured tanks

Dominie – vicar, minister of religion

Great Trek – mass emigration of settlers, mainly of Dutch origin, from the Cape of Good Hope in the 1830's

Kaffir – lit. (from Arabic) non-believer, pejorative name for African

Kraal – African village, a group of huts or a cattle enclosure

Laager – defensive fortification formed by circle of wagons – sometimes used to describe mentality of Afrikaners reluctant to integrate

Mealie meal – maize finely ground which forms staple diet for Africans

Pap – mealie meal porridge

Rondavel – African round hut

Sjambok – heavy wooden baton used as a weapon, similar to knobkerries

Verkrampte – reactionary, hardliner

Verligte – enlightened, moderate

Volk – people